CONTENTS

News from the Seat of War, *a watercolour by Gourlay Steele showing Highland soldiers leaving for the Crimea, 1855.* NMS

THE THISTLE AT WAR

An anthology of the Scottish experience of
war, in the services and at home

Edited by Helen McCorry

Introduction by Eric Lomax

NATIONAL MUSEUMS OF SCOTLAND

Published by National Museums of Scotland Publishing,
Chambers Street, Edinburgh EH1 1JF

© Trustees of the National Museums of Scotland 1997.
Introduction © Eric Lomax

British Library Cataloguing in Publication Data

A catalogue record of this book is available from the British
Library

ISBN 0 948636 91 2

Designed by National Museums of Scotland Publishing

Printed by Magnum International Printing Co Ltd, Hong
Kong

*Cover image: Piper George Clark of the 71st (Highland)
Regiment of Foot, although wounded in the legs and unable to
stand, continues to play the pipes to encourage his comrades at
the Battle of Vimiera, Portugal, 1808.* NMS

INTRODUCTION

The Scots have been at war, in one form or another, for a very long time. Sometimes this activity has been directed at an outside enemy, sometimes against an enemy at home, sometimes both at once.

Perhaps the earliest great battle in Scotland was at Mons Graupius, in AD 84. Though we do not know where the place was, we do know that tens of thousands of wild men, the predecessors of the later Scots, put a stop to the northward expansion of the Roman Empire.

Stories have long been told of how a complete Roman legion, the Ninth, subsequently marched from Eboracum (York) into Caledonia round about AD 117 in order to deal with these same ferocious men. The Ninth Legion was said to have vanished, never to be heard of again. The assumption has always been that the tribesmen in the Northern mists were able to dispose of a unit of 5000 highly trained Romans without leaving any traces. While the story is now completely discounted, the reputation of the early Scots survives.

Battles with marauding Vikings took place throughout the centuries, until Scotland achieved a degree of unification under the first Kings of Scots in the ninth century.

From ancient times, and indeed until comparatively recently, groups of Scots gathered together into fighting units only for a particular campaign or for a specific purpose, perhaps to defend a locality against a threat of invasion. Sometimes these men were paid, sometimes not. In parallel with this, many thousands of Scotsmen joined foreign armies, mainly on the Continent, and served in some remarkable foreign campaigns.

Gradually the informal forces were replaced by formal organisations. Following, first, the Union of the Crowns and, second, the Commonwealth the beginnings of a permanent standing army can be found in the creation in 1661, under Charles II of 'His Majesty's Guards and Garrisons'. Who has not heard of the Coldstream Guards, the Scots Guards and the Royal Scots? The Royal Scots, sometimes referred to as Pontius Pilate's Bodyguard, is a regiment of great antiquity.

While the Union of England and Scotland nominally reduced the need for large standing forces, the last battles on British soil took place in

Scotland itself. Charles Edward Stuart, in the early months of the 'Forty Five' and on his march south, defeated Government forces at Prestonpans. After a reverse at Derby and a long retreat north, the Jacobite cause was finally extinguished at Culloden on 17 September 1746, the last battle of all. Thereafter there has been peace within England and Scotland, relatively speaking.

Warfare for many centuries was entirely a land affair. Occasional skirmishes with invaders arriving by sea certainly occurred from time to time but warfare at sea was not very practicable until the creation by James IV of the Scots Navy. Probably the King's greatest naval achievement was the building of his ship the *Michael*, popularly known as the *Great Michael*. Launched at Newhaven in 1511 the *Great Michael* was probably the largest ship in the world at the time, with a crew of 300 and accommodation for 1000 soldiers.

Strictly speaking, however, this book is not concerned with the history or the development of warfare involving Scotsmen and the Scottish services. There are many such texts. This book is a collection of first-hand personal accounts of the experiences of Scottish servicemen in a variety of wars and situations through the ages. It extends from Bannockburn in 1314 to the fight for recognition and compensation by the 1990-91 Gulf War veterans in 1997. This last campaign on the part of those concerned with Gulf War syndrome has developed almost into a war in its own right, the opposing forces being the veterans themselves and the Ministry of Defence. At the time of writing it looks as though the Gulf War veterans will win.

Written records of and by individual soldiers in the earlier centuries are almost non-existent. Important but relevant documents can be found from as early as the thirteenth century or so, however, increasing in quantity and variety to the present day. The language used in much of the earlier autobiographical writing may present some readers with problems but the glossary will help. That interpretation is still a real problem, even in Scotland, can be seen in a historical work recently published in Edinburgh in which the author, commenting on Sir Patrick Spens, mistranslates 'Haf owre, haf owre to Aberdour' as 'A half-hour from Aberdour'!

For reasons which we need not go into at the moment my personal emotions were buried many years ago. It is thus a great compliment to the late-lamented David Niven that when I first read *The Moon's a Balloon*, the tears came into my eyes over the amazing description of an incident in the departure of The Highland Light infantry from Valletta, Malta in the 1930s. Where else has an entire infantry battalion diverted itself from the official line of route so that *Scotland the Brave* could be heard, for the last time, by a Company Sergeant Major terminally ill in hospital? David Niven has given us a magnificent piece of writing in his account of leaving Malta. It is in this volume.

There is also a fascinating reference to the celebrated visit to Derby by the Jacobite army, in 1745. Where else have the local landladies expressed their fears that the Highland men ate children? Then there is a splendid traditional account of Highland Second Sight. There is also a curious little account of how the ancient Athole Highlanders 'volunteered' for service.

In complete contrast there is a strange and fascinating little piece about the superb elegance of a French woman travelling in a cattle truck on a wartime train.

I commend specially the extract from *Voices from War*, drawing attention to the problem of interpreting the magic initials C O. Many of us have been caught out over this!

There is a striking story in this book, too, of how three young women, abandoned by their soldier lovers, walked daily from Edinburgh to Leith harbour, to load and unload coal, in 1804. They were said to have walked barefoot. Young ladies would grumble today, if they had to do this when short of funds. Perhaps some readers will readily understand the piece in which are outlined the perils of allowing a Regiment to become 'encumbered with women'!

Almost the last item, an account of problems left over from soldiering in Burma in the Second World War, may seem far fetched. I confirm its terrible authenticity.

Eric Lomax

God save great George our King

An Old PERFORMER playing on a New INSTRUMENT.
or one of the 42.ᵈ Touching the Invincible

'DID ANYONE EVER HIT YE AFORE, SERGEANT?'

Scots and Scottishness

A French view

The Scots are a bold, hardy people, very experienced in war. At that time they had little love or respect for the English and the same is true today.

Jean Froissart *Chronicles, 1523-25*

Shylock's observation, Venice, 1597

Some men there are love not a gaping pig;
Some, that are mad if they behold a cat;
And others, when the bagpipe sings i' the nose,
Cannot contain their urine.

William Shakespeare *The Merchant of Venice*

The Scots as cannibals, Derby, 1745

One evening, as Mr Cameron of Locheil entered the lodgings assigned him, his landlady, an old woman, threw herself at his feet, and with uplifted hands, and tears in her eyes, supplicated him to take her life, but to spare her two little children. He asked her if she was in her senses, and told her to explain herself, when she answered, that *everybody said that the Highlanders ate children and made them their common food.* Mr Cameron having assured her that they would not injure either her or her little children, or any person whatever, she looked at him for some moments with an air of surprise, and then opened a press, calling out with a loud voice: 'Come out, children, the gentleman will not eat you'.

The Chevalier de Johnstone *Memoirs of the rebellion in 1745, 1746*

An Old Performer playing on a New Instrument, *a soldier of the 42nd Regiment plays Napoleon like a set of bagpipes: this refers to the resumption of hostilities after the failure of the Peace of Amiens, 1803.* NMS

Ticonderoga, 1758

This is one of the best-authenticated tales of Highland second sight, being in circulation well before the final event took place.

In the summer of 1755, Major Duncan Campbell of Inverawe was walking on Ben Cruachan when he encountered a frightened and dishevelled figure who sought his protection, saying that he had unintentionally killed a man and was hiding from the man's friends. Campbell agreed to help him, but the man insisted that he take an oath to this effect on his dirk: the Highlander was offended that his word should not be enough and swore 'by the word of an Inverawe, which never yet failed friend or foe'.

He took the runaway to a safe spot and returned home, to find that the man who had died was his own foster brother. He stuck by his oath to the fugitive, but the spirit of his murdered brother appeared to him the following two nights, covered in blood, and said, 'Inverawe, shield not the murderer. Blood must flow for blood.' On the third day, Campbell showed the fugitive an escape route and his brother appeared that night to say, 'Farewell, Inverawe, till we meet at Ticonderoga.'

When Campbell went to North America three years later as an officer in the Black Watch, he told this story to his brother officers and repeatedly reminded them to tell him if they heard the place name. In fact, the fort was then more generally known by the name of Fort Carillon. On the eve of battle the spirit of his murdered brother visited Campbell in his tent again and in the morning he told the others 'This is Ticonderoga. I shall die today.' And he did.

Traditional

The Scots and the Spaniards, Bejar, 1813

I got a most excellent billet. Everything was in plenty, fruit in abundance. I was regarded as a son of the family, partook with them at meals and, if anything was better than another, my part was in it. I amused myself, when off duty, in teaching the children to read, for which my hosts thought they never could be grateful enough.

I have often thought the Spaniards resembled the Scots in their manner of treating their children. How has my heart warmed, when I have seen the father, with his wife by his side, and the children round them, repeating the Lord's prayer and the 23rd Psalm at evening before they went to bed. Once a week the children were catechised. When I told them they did the same in Scotland they looked at me with astonishment, and asked 'If heretics did so?' The priests often drew comparisons much to our disadvantage from the conduct of our men. They even said every heretic in England was as bad as them.

Journal of a soldier of the 71st regiment

The opinion of a trooper in the Royal Scots Greys, 1832

Tell the young Scotchman who recites the glories of his favourite Greys while he rests on the harvest field with listening shearers all around, or when he listens in the charmed crowd in the village smithy to the veteran who is village smith now, but who was a farrier in the regiment once, that the Greys did *not* do the whole of Waterloo; that they did *not* win all nor any of 'Lord Wallinton's' battles in the Peninsular War, inasmuch as they were not in the Peninsula; that the Highland regiments were not the regiments '*always* in front of Wallinton's battles'; tell the young Scotchman, or the old one either, the historical truth, that the 42nd Highlanders were not slain at Quatre Bras, on the 16th of June, through their impetuous bravery, but through the irregularity of their movements, whereby, in forming square to receive cavalry, two companies were shut out and *skivered* by Marshal Ney and the French

Watercolour showing NCOs and men of the Royal Scots Greys in Ireland, c1848, by Michael Angelo Hayes. NMS

Watercolour of Lord Arthur Hill, Lieutenant-Colonel commanding the Royal Scots Greys, 1834, by Master F Frith, aged 15. NMS

dragoons; tell him that more reports were circulated in newspapers during the war, setting forth the superior achievements of the Scotch regiments - those reports still existing in tradition - through the Scotch soldiers being nearly all able to write letters home to their friends, while very few of the English or Irish soldiers could write home to their friends, there being no parochial schools in England or Ireland as there are in Scotland; tell the young Scotchman at the smithy-door all or any of these things, especially the last, that it was the *writing* quite as much as the *fighting* of the Scotch regiments that distinguished them, and he will tell you that you are no Scotchman; that you are not worthy of having such regiments as the 'Heelant Watch' (42nd), or the 'Gallant Greys'.

Alexander Somerville *Autobiography of a working man*

An outside view, World War I

Evidence is more plentiful for the rather more numerous Scots, not least in the comments of the Dominion troops. Whereas the Anzacs were contemptuous and pitying towards the 'Tommy', they admired 'the Jocks' and recognized a 'kinship' with them. Fellow-feeling may have played a part in the Etaples mutiny, where 'the presence of both Scottish and Anzac ... soldiers gave the mutiny a cohesiveness which a riot could not otherwise have attained'.

In Palestine too, Scots and Anzacs together were responsible for the worst breach of discipline in the theatre, when they descended upon the Arab village of Surafend in bloody reprisal for the shooting of a New Zealander. Specifically, their comradeship was founded upon an affinity of spirit, the Australians seeing their own vigorous egalitarianism reflected in the Scottish troops' 'independent stalwart outlook' and 'rugged sincerity'. In contrast, the Tommies' unquestioning acceptance of authority was a subject for parody.

The evidence of the mutinies, scanty as it is, suggests that there was some foundation for the idea of a similarity between Scots and Australians. In the two wartime base mutinies, it was the men of the 51st (Highland) Division who staged the Calais disturbance, while at Etaples it was the shooting of a man of the 1/4th Battalion Gordon Highlanders which sparked the rioting, and 'if the insubordination of the Anzacs played an important part on the first day of the mutiny, it was the Scottish troops, present in far greater numbers, who gave the mutiny its force'. Curiously, in the Second World War too, it was men of the 51st Division, together with others from the 50th (Northumbrian), who were to be responsible for the largest and best-known British mutiny of that conflict, at Salerno in 1943.

J G Fuller *Troop morale and popular culture*

The back of this photograph of two smiling Scots Guards reads, 'Belgium, 1944. Love from Jimmy and Bob'. Robert Maguire is on the right. Dr Louise Maguire

An Italian Scottish Nationalist, 1940

Anyhow when we arrived at York racecourse - it wasn't long before Christmas 1940 - we were hungry, tired, cold - a drizzly day. There was barbed wire round a big encampment, where the tote and things were. We got into single file and here was an officer with a table and then you passed on from him to the camp. So when I came up to him, he says: 'What's your ... ? 'I'm C 98.' 'Giuseppe Pia?' 'Yes.' He says, Well, nationality English, of course.' I says, 'I beg your pardon?' He says, 'Your nationality is English.' I says, 'I'm not English,' I said, 'there's nothing English about me.' I says, 'I'm Scottish or British, if you like, or even Italian. I'm of dual nationality, British-Italian. Put down either Italian, British or Scottish but certainly not English.' He says, 'I've got to write down English.' I says, 'Oh yes? But I'm not an Englishman. So you can't mark English for me.' And all the others in the queue are saying, 'Oh, what's this?', you see. And of course naturally I've held up the queue: 'What is it? What is it?' 'I don't know.' 'Oh.' 'I wonder what that chap's doing?', you see. Here's a big crowd - two or three hundred people (there were only 400 in the camp) - so half of them were all excited, wondering what the hang's wrong. Anything for excitement, you see. But the chap behind me says, 'Oh, shut your mouth, Joe! Let him write down everything. What difference does it make? I'm tired, I'm cold, I'm hungry.' So I says, 'All right then, go and shove it down.' So here I go forward, but quite annoyed, you see. And of course in the camp: 'What is it?' I says, 'He wants to put me down as an Englishman! There's nothing English about me! I'm a Scot, not an Englishman!' And I'm shouting, quite annoyed. 'Oh, are you?' And of course the word flashes right down. So here before I know it, a chap comes across to me, shakes hands, and claps me on the back: 'Well done! Well done! Your name's Joe, isn't it?' I says, 'Yes.' 'Well done!' I says, 'By the

way, who are you?' 'Oh, my name's Hamish Hamilton.' 'Hamish Hamilton?' I says. 'Why are you here?' 'Oh,' he says, 'I'm a Scots Nationalist.' I says, 'A Scots Nationalist?' 'Yes,' he says, 'oh, they consider we're anti-war as well. There are four of us in the camp are Scots Nationalists.' I says, 'Is that so?' He says, 'Oh, yes, and we've got Irish and Welsh Nationalists here as well.' 'Is that so?' And I says, 'And you are a Scots Nationalist?' He says, 'Yes.' I says, 'By the way, don't tell me that you let them write down that you're English?' 'Oh, well,' he says, 'what else could you do?' I says, 'Well, I mean, I've never bothered about nationality in my life before. But, I mean, you a Scots Nationalist letting them write down "English"? I who am not a nationalist make a fuss about being called English and you make no bother at all?' 'Oh, well,' he says, 'you have to do it, you know what I mean.'

Joseph Pia, in Ian MacDougall *Voices from war*

Piper Muir of the 42nd (Royal Highlanders) after his return from the Crimea, 1856. 'He's beezed himself up for a photy an a', as Hamish Henderson was to write almost 100 years later. NMS

A wild man, a head case

Nothing put more heart in me, young and unsure as I was - most of all, fearful of being seen to be fearful - than the fact that, being a Scot, it was half expected of me that I would be a wild man, a head case. This age-old belief among the English, that their northern neighbours are desperate fellows, hangs on, and whether it's true or not it's one hell of an encouragement when you're nineteen and wondering how you'll be when the whistle blows and you take a deep breath and push your safety catch forward.

George MacDonald Fraser *Quartered safe out here*

George Campbell Hay in a letter home to Douglas Young, 1941

Luckily the NCOs are decent souls, including our own Sergeant, one algar [sic], a Geordie from near Alnwick who had the pleasure of being carted thro' Dunkirk as a casualty from Flanders. As he is from the North and speaks what is almost a kind of Lallans I can understand him when he opens his mouth. But some of the NCOS (only the CSM and one sergeant are Scots) are a continuous puzzle to their men, and vice versa. One corporal told his platoon that the first letter of the alphabet was 'Oi' (or more 'oi'). On the other hand a quiet soul of 39 years from the Broch went and asked his sergeant if he would 'bide ahint' where we paraded. The funniest instance of language fog was caused by a Glesca boy who, being a great consumer of beer, was puffing and panting at PT and screwing up his face in anguish. 'Wot are you pantin' and makin' fices for?' asked the instructor. 'If you don't loike to be 'ere we don't want cher.' When Glesca had interpreted this to himself he was deeply insulted and howled 'Ah wisnie mekin' faces ah wiz pechin'. The instructor gazed blankly at him, but was too mindful of his dignity to ask what 'pechin' meant.

Ink and watercolour sketch entitled Appearing before an officer, *by F C B Cadell, 1915.*

The Caledonians and South Britons mix no better than oil and water. If you ask about anyone and what sort of person he is the first classification is always 'He's wan o they bloody Englishmen' or 'He's a Scotch bastard' and that's the natural attitude you get. If you strike up an acquaintance with an Englishman (excepting a small minority) you feel it's abnormal and provisional. The most noticeable characteristic about the English is how docile they are, and it's not a docility with after-thoughts and reservations. But most of my compatriots, God be thankit, haven't the faintest trace of the spirit of subordination and they are incredibly outspoken for poor bloody privates. A Fifeman I know well (a piper) once caught one of the Regimental Police washing with the official armband of authority off. 'Ye ken' he said to him 'ye're a dour sort of bugger'. 'I don't understand you Scotch people', said the dumbfounded RP. 'What do you mean, I'm dour?' 'I mean ye're an awfu' sulky kinna bugger'. 'I'm not sulky' (he must have been thrown quite off his balance to demean himself by going into explanations) 'I've got a lot of worries on my shoulders.' 'Ach, I hae mair worries in the arse of my troosers'. One Aberdonian (we have plenty) eyed a nagging kind of sergeant significantly and said 'Did anyone ever hit ye afore, sergeant?'

George Campbell Hay

Some people want to be Scottish even if they aren't

Lieutenant Colonel Jack Churchill, who has died aged 89, was probably the most dramatically impressive Commando leader of the Second World War. His exploits - charging up beaches dressed only in a kilt and brandishing a dirk, killing with a bow and arrow, playing the bagpipes at moments of extreme peril - and his legendary escapes won him the admiration and devotion of those under his command, who nicknamed him 'Mad Jack'.

Churchill believed that an assault leader should have a reputation which would demoralise the enemy and convince his own men that nothing was impossible. He was awarded two DSOs and an MC, and mentioned in despatches.

John Malcolm Thorpe Fleming Churchill was born in Surrey on 16 September 1906. After education at the Dragon School, Oxford, King William's College, Isle of Man, and Sandhurst, Churchill was commissioned into the Manchester Regiment and gazetted to the 2nd Battalion, which he joined in Rangoon. At Maymyo he learned to play the bagpipes, tutored by the Pipe Major of the Cameron Highlanders, and became an outstanding performer. But when the regiment returned to Britain in 1936, he became bored with military life at the depot at Ashton-under-Lyne and retired after only 10 years in the Army.

On the outbreak of war in 1939, he was recalled to the Colours and went to France... After returning to England, he joined the Commandos and in 1941 was Second in Command of a mixed force from 2 and 3 Commandos which raided Vaagso in Norway. Before landing, Churchill decided to look the part. He wore silver buttons he had acquired in France; carried his bow and arrows and armed himself with a broadhilted claymore; and led the landing force ashore with his bagpipes. Although he was again wounded, the operation forced the Germans to concentrate large forces in the area.

After recovering, Churchill was appointed Lieutenant Colonel commanding No 2 Commando which he took through Sicily (leading with his bagpipes to Messina) and then to the landings at Salerno. They captured the village of Pigoletti and its garrison of 42 men as well as an 81 mm mortar and its crew. In further fighting along the Pigoletti Ridge, he was recommended for the VC but eventually received the DSO. His action had saved the Salerno beachhead at a critical time.

From 'The Highlander', 1996

Hal o' the Wynd

Hal o' the Wynd he taen the field
Alang be the skinklin Tay:
And he hackit doun the men o' Chattan;
Or was it the men o' Kay?

Whan a' was owre he dichted his blade
And steppit awa richt douce
To draik his drouth in the Skinners' Vennel
At clapperin Clemmy's house.

Hal o' the Wynd had monie a bairn;
And bairns' bairns galore
Wha wud speer about the bluidy battle
And what it was fochten for.

'Guid-faith! my dawties, I never kent;
But yon was a dirlin' day
Whan I hackit doun the men o' Chattan;
Or was it the men o' Kay?'

William Soutar (1898-1943)

Taking it seriously

Scotsmen, of course, if they feel their national prestige is in any way at stake, tend to go out of their minds; tell them there was to be a knitting-bee against England and they would be on the touchline shouting, "Purl, Wullie! See's the chain-stitch, but!"

George MacDonald Fraser *McAuslan in the rough*

KIT AND KILTS

Uniform, boots, and, most particularly, feet

A fine pair of boots, 1745

After Culloden one of Cumberland's troopers was ambushed by a MacRae piper, who then took a liking to the dead man's boots. But however hard he pulled the boots would not come off, so in the end he severed the legs at the knees and wrapped them up in his plaid. Arriving at Torghoil, the piper was given food and refreshment, and then settled down in the byre next to a brindled cow. During the night he managed to extract the legs from the boots, and he went off early in the morning leaving the limbs behind. When the maid came to wake him she was horrified at what she saw, and ran screaming to the house: 'The brindled cow has eaten the piper, all but his two feet.' So the innkeeper came out with an axe, killed the cow, and buried her and the Englishman's legs in the same grave.

Traditional

Colonel Cameron's opinion of trews

Glasgow, 27th October, 1804

Sir,

On my return hither some days ago from Stirling, I received your letter of 13th Inst (by General Calvert's orders) respecting the propriety of an alteration of the mode in clothing Highland regiments, in reply to which I beg to state, freely and fully, my sentiments upon that subject, without a particle of prejudice in either way, but merely founded on *facts* applicable to these corps - at least as far as I am *capable*, from thirty years' experience, twenty years of which have been upon *actual* service in all *climates*, with the description of men in question, which independent of myself being a Highlander, and well knowing all the convenience and inconvenience of our native garb in the field and otherwise, and perhaps, also, aware of the probable source and clashing motives from which the suggestion now under consideration originally arose. I have to observe progressively, that in course of the late war several gentlemen proposed to raise Highland regiments - some for general service, but chiefly for home defence; but most of these corps were called upon from all quarters, and thereby adulterated by every description of men that rendered them anything but real Highlanders, or even, Scotchmen (which is not strictly synonymous): and the colonels themselves being generally unacquainted with the language and habits of Highlanders while prejudiced in favour of, and accustomed to wear, breeches, consequently *adverse* to that free congenial circulation of that pure wholesome air (as an exhilarating native bracer) which has hitherto so peculiarly benefited the Highlander for *activity* and all the other necessary qualities of a soldier, whether for hardship upon scanty fare, *readiness in accoutring*, or making *forced marches*, - besides the exclusive advantage, when halted, of drenching his kilt in the *next brook* as well as washing his limbs and drying *both*, as it were by constant *fanning*, without injury to either, but, on the contrary, feeling clean and comfortable; whilst the buffoon tartan pantaloon, with its fringed frippery (as some mongrel Highlanders would have it), sticking wet and dirty to the skin, is not very easily pulled off, and *less so* to get on again in case of alarm or any other hurry and all this time absorbing both wet and dirt, followed by rheumatism and fevers, which alternately make great havoc in hot and cold climates; while it consists with knowledge that the Highlander in his native garb always appeared more cleanly and maintained proper health in both climates, than those who wore even the thick cloth pantaloons.

Print of a Highland soldier in North America, possibly an advertisement for tobacco and snuff, c1790. NMS

Alan Cameron of Erracht, Colonel of the 79th regiment, Cameron Highlanders
Historical Records of the Cameron Highlanders

Foreign fops and antiquated prigs, Musselburgh, 1805

During the time the regiment was quartered in Musselburgh, a general order was issued for the army to discontinue the tying of the hair, and to have it cropped. Never was an order received with more heartfelt satisfaction than this, or obeyed with more alacrity, notwithstanding the foolish predictions of some old superannuated gentlemen, that it would cause a mutiny in the army. The tying was a daily penance, and a severe one, to which every man had to submit; and there is little doubt, but this practice had been introduced by some foreign fops, and enforced by antiquated prigs, as necessary to the cleanly appearance of the soldier. It had been very injurious in its effects on the general comforts of those who were obliged to submit to it, and the soldier looks back to the task with the painful remembrance of the punishment he suffered every morning, daubing the side of his head with dirty grease, soap, and flour, until every hair stood like the burr of a thistle, and the back was padded and pulled so, that every hair had to keep its due place; if one less subordinate than the rest chanced to start up in spite of grease, soap-lather, and flour, the poor man had to sit down and submit his head to another dressing, and afterwards parade for inspection among the defaulters of the regiment. A certain latitude and longitude was assigned for the breadth and length of the queue, to which a gauge was frequently applied, in the same manner as some modern sticklers for uniformity, to this day, use a measure to ascertain the dimensions of the soldiers' folded greatcoats at guard-mounting; but with this difference, the coat receives no bad impression from the stickler's gauge, whereas the greased and powdered hair retained the mark, and the poor fellow who had the misfortune to have the powder brushed aside by his awkward inspector, stood a chance of being turned off parade to have his hair dressed afresh, just as if the unlucky mark rendered him unfit for any military movement, or divested him of all the requisites of a soldier.

Indeed, it was no uncommon occurrence for us, when on the guard-bench and asleep, to have the rats and mice scrambling about our heads, eating the filthy stuff with which our hair was bedaubed. We now look back to that time with a feeling of contempt at the absurdity of that detestable custom, and bless the memory of that prince who emancipated us from such an annoying and filthy practice.

James Anton *Retrospect of a military life*

Highland bonnets of the 71st in Spain, 1808

One day a party of our men was sent down to protect the embarkation of some sick and wounded French from the ruthless violence of a Portugueze mob. During the whole of our stay in the park, the city was illuminated every night, on account, I presume, of the expulsion of the Gallic invaders. The ostrich feathers on our Highland bonnets had become so much the admiration of the Portugueze ladies, that no less than a dollar was offered for each of them by the hawkers about the camp; and this induced some villains amongst us to rob their comrades. I suffered in this way, in common with some others, having my bonnet completely plucked while I was asleep. Instead of receiving even commiseration for my loss, I was compelled to pay

2*l.* sterling for a new bonnet, and was in danger of being flogged besides: such is military justice!

Several deserters came over here from the French army to the British. They were of different nations, Swiss, Germans, and Italians; nearly the whole of them, about twenty in number, chose to enlist in our regiment, I know not for what reason, (as every corps in our army was open to them,) unless the wearing of tartan was considered as a fine thing by these mercenary fellows.

Vicissitudes in the life of a Scottish soldier

Welcome home after Corunna, 1809

We were not long till we came in sight of Ramsgate. I left my old firelock with the sailors. But in preparing to leave the ship, I went to my knapsack to put on my new shoes that I got when I came to Corunna, but to my sad disappointment they were stolen away by someone. When I landed, the regiment was on parade ready to march off for Canterbury. We joined our company with the same

THE GREAT AND THE SMALL ARE THERE

appearance as we came from Corunna. We marched off, and it was not long before it came on very wet. I went forward as well as I could, but my old shoes would not keep on my feet. I had then to take them off. I did the best I could for some time, but had to fall out of the ranks. A Corporal was ordered to go with me. The people were looking at the regiment passing, but when they saw me I was looked upon as an object of pity. Well might they say here is a representative of what we have heard about Corunna retreat. I was stopped; shoes and stockings were brought to me, and as I was putting them on, they were asking questions about me at the Corporal, for he was a country man of their own. The English showed no small kindness to the soldiers that came from Corunna. When they came into the towns after marching, some of the people took them to their houses without billets. We came away, and I was very thankful for the kindness shewed to me.

Bugler John Macfarlane *Peninsular private*

The Great and the Small, *by John Kay, shows Major-General Roger Aytoun, who was six feet four, with the Duc d'Angouleme, who was five feet four, in 1797. The Duc d'Angouleme resided at Holyrood Palace in Edinburgh for some years after the French Revolution. In the background is the 1st Regiment of Edinburgh Volunteers.* NMS

The Black Watch after Waterloo, December 1815

On the 2d December the frost set in with unusual severity: the cold was more like that of the polar regions than of France. Our Highlanders had their flesh laid open and bleeding, by the ruffling of the kilts against their thighs; the icicles gathered in clusters at our eyebrows, and the whiskered men appeared as if they had been powdered by some hairdresser; but we had no sickness. We rested two nights in Abbeville, and a fall of snow relaxed the intensity of the cold.

James Anton *Retrospect of a military life*

Getting dressed in the Royal Scots Greys, 1832

The troop sergeant-major, to whom I was allotted, brought me a forage cap, a leather stock, four linen shirts, two flannel waistcoats, two pair of flannel drawers, four pairs of worsted socks, two pairs of gloves, a pair of gauntlets (gloves reaching to the elbows), a curry comb and brushes, a horse's mane comb, sponges, soap, bath brick, save-all, with knife, fork, spoon, razor, comb, shaving tackle, two towels, turn-screw, picker (for horse's feet), button stick, button brush, rot-stone to clean buttons, boot brushes, blacking, clothes brush, brush bag, horse's nose bag, corn sack, horse cloth (the cover for the stable); account book with printed regulations, saddle bags, military cloak, and two pairs of straps for overalls (trousers), which he proceeded to show me how to affix to the buttons. 'Now, my man,' he proceeded to say, 'One of the first things a young soldier must learn is the proper way of dressing himself, and he must do it very quickly. You will occasionally find that every article of your clothing and accoutrements must be put on in a minute of time, and your horse accoutred, turned out, and mounted in another minute; I am serious with you; such a thing will require to be done, though not always. But to be able to do it at any time, you must practise yourself to put everything on and off in the proper way, in the briefest space of time. For instance, your straps; there is a right way and a wrong way of fastening them, and you are proceeding in the wrong way. Here, turn the outside of your foot upward; button the strap to that side first; turn the inside of your foot up next, and now bring it under your sole and fasten it to the inside. Now you do it right; the other one do in the same way - *that's* right; you will be a soldier in no time. Now, the stock about your neck; why you have buckled it behind already. Ah! I see you'll get on. Button up your coatee; hook the collar; draw down the skirts; throw out your chest; no, not your stomach, draw *that* in; throw back your shoulders; up your head - up yet; don't throw your head

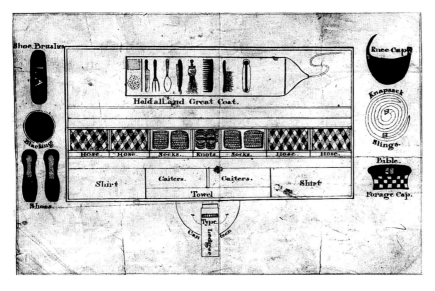

back; stretch it upright; don't bend your knees - stretch your knees; put the forage cap a little to the right side; bring it a little over the right eyebrow - not quite so much; now the strap down upon your chin, not under the chin; let it come just under your lip. Now, look at yourself in the glass. Don't be afraid to look at yourself in a glass; I like a soldier who looks at himself in a glass; he is never a dirty soldier. Don't laugh at yourself. What do you see in the glass to laugh at? you only see yourself; and you will get used to yourself. But I was like you; I laughed too when I saw myself in regimentals first.' And to this effect he continued to explain my duty, in a manner exceedingly kind and encouraging.

Alexander Somerville *Autobiography of a working man*

Benefits of the kilt, circa 1900

The wonder is that I saw anyone. The whisky was followed by champagne, and the champagne by beer, and I soon became intolerably garrulous, to the well-disguised alarm of Iain Murray's party. By midnight I was feeling very strange indeed, and at about that time went down to the men's room. I found it deserted except for a middle-aged major of Highlanders. He was holding up the front of his kilt with one hand and leaning against the wall. He turned to me while in this position and said portentously, 'Join a Highland regiment, me boy. The kilt is an unrivalled garment for fornication and diarrhoea.'

John Masters *Bugles and a tiger*

Elegance under pressure, World War II

Out of the medley of memories three incidents stand out more clearly than the rest. One was when, to André's huge delight, we had to do part of our journey in an open cattle-truck. By that stage we were all looking pretty bedraggled, and André was so filthy that I doubt whether I would have had the courage to touch him if he had been someone else's child. We had therefore little to lose when we settled ourselves as comfortably as we could on the floor of our cattle-truck. We were joined there by a lady from St Germain-en-Laye. She was like a breath from Paris. Though she sat on the floor with us she never lost her air of neat elegance, and the sight of her struck guilt to my soul, for it reminded me that I had been taking advantage of circumstances to let my standards down, an unpardonable thing in France. This lady was dressed in a beautiful black tailor-made suit, a white lingerie blouse that was still really white, and a small black hat which could only have come from Paris. Her one concession to the occasion was a pair of rather old brown court shoes, but I felt certain, as certain as though I had peeped inside, that in the little dressing-case she carried with her there was another pair of shoes, black and well-polished, and that she would change into them the moment she was near her destination.

Janet Teissier du Cros *Divided loyalties*

Another Highland opinion of trews, 1942

We arrived at a battalion encamped near the airport at Daba. It was resting after Alamein and Rear Division had sent us as reinforcements. An officers' mess tent had been erected and we were introduced to the officers of the battalion as they came in for tea. They received us with courteous smiles and frigid behaviour. The Commanding Officer greeted us exquisitely and distantly. We were not, it was enquired politely, commissioned into their regiment? We were not entitled to wear their badge? No, we replied, we were officers of other regiments, but Rear Division had sent us as reinforcements. They smiled again, silently, and their politeness became even colder. We were strangers to their particular tradition, foreigners who were not permitted to wear the tartan of their design.

After tea we walked over the desert to where our bed-rolls were lying on the sand. There was a small bivouac nearby, inhabited by the adjutant. We went there to make an issue of this regimental tradition which sneered at reinforcements whose cap badges did not carry the correct Gaelic motto.

As we came near the tent we heard the adjutant speaking on the field telephone. "Hello, hello, is that Rear Div? Look here, about those officers you sent us. Yes, they're here. But the Old Man says he made it perfectly clear that he has no use for people who are not commissioned into this regiment. He says he won't keep them. They don't even wear kilts but those tartan trouser things. Shall I send them back? No, quite definitely he doesn't want them."

We walked away unobserved and sat on our bed-rolls. On the far side of the airport, with its smashed burned-out planes, there was a road on which transport was moving, bringing up the supplies of war. In the past few months Australians, Greeks, Canadians, South Africans, French, had been fighting together in this country. Yet we were now bumping against a clan system which had been nominally destroyed by Butcher Cumberland in 1746. We had discovered in a twentieth-century Armageddon a Highland Lieutenant-Colonel, desperate for reinforcements to replace his killed and wounded officers, who would not allow Lowland Scots to fight beside him. And the half-colonel spoke with the accents of Mayfair.

Neil McCallum *Journey with a pistol*

Mrs Doreen Butler, née Bell, in her Land Army uniform, 1941.
Scottish Life Archive

Dancing in uniform, 1942

The Land Army supplied an awful uniform. Do you remember footballers wearing long shorts to their knees, how drab, how awful they looked? Well our uniform wasn't cut short at the knee, but it had that same sort of dreariness. A sort of khaki overall and puttees, a word which nowadays nobody understands. And we had a badge, and some awful kind of felt hat with no shape. But a cousin of mine had a pair of riding breeches with smart suede knee patches and they fitted me. So when I was off duty I used to go up to London and dance at the Berkeley and places like that in my chic uniform.

The first time I was taken to the Berkeley Hotel, they wouldn't let me in. A chap I was with, a Scottie wearing tartan trews, made a fuss. 'You let me in, so let her in. She's in uniform like all the services.' They did at last, and of course I was much admired for my patriotic war work.

Kathleen Hale, in Mavis Nicholson
What did you do in the war, Mummy?

A SHILLING A DAY
Recruitment, conscription and rank

Serjeant John Wilson enlists in 1695

Before I Enter upon the Particulars of the Ensueing Journall, I think it not amiss to give my Reader an Accot of my first Entering into the Army, and Regiment aforesaid, then comanded by Sr. James Lessley; I Entered as a Soldier with Ensigne William Haliday to serve in the Regiment aforesaid upon the 25th day of March 1694, and came to the Regiment then Quartered in the Cannongate Edenburgh the day following, and the next day was Shewn to Sr. James with Severall Other Recruits. Upon Sr. James's takeing a veiw of me, he was pleased to Say to Ensigne Haliday, What my friend Haliday do you bring me Children for Soldiers, I did not Expect this from You, for You know Wee want men, Ensigne Haliday answered in an Humble Manner, that he must Confess I was too Young, but that it was Intirely my own Desire and that my Parents Could not diswade me from it, therefore they were Desireous I should be under His Honours Care, whereupon Sr. James Askt Whose Childe I was and if he had any knowledge of my parents, The Ensigne told Sr. James my fathers name, whom Sr. James knew, and Said he knew my Grandfather also, whereupon Sr. James turned to me with a frown, and Said, You Young Rogue how came you to Run away from yor Parents. I answered him I did not run away, but came with their Consent to be a Soldier. A Soldier Says Sr. James with a Smileing Countenance, go home you Young rogue and go to School, to which En's Haliday made answer and said Sr., if you turn him back he will Certainly go with some other recruiting Officer, and that would very much Vex his parents, - Then Sr. James said, I should go home upon ffurloe, and lett him have three months pay advance, and his ffurloe for a full year, both of wch I had next morning, and comitted to the Charge of En's Halidays Brother to See me Safe home, wch the Gentleman performed, and I went again to School and continued till Such time as I broke up for Christmass, at wch time En's Haliday came from Flanders to Scottland in order to raise Recruits, I being Informed of his Arrival at his Brothers in the Evening, went The next morning like a Dutifull Soldier to wait upon my Officer, desired one of his Brothers Servts to acquaint him I was Come to wait his Commands, and he ordered the Servt to bidd me come up to him, and I imediatly went up to his Chamber, he asked me very kindly how I did, and Whether I continu'd my Resolution of going Abroad, I answered Yes Sr., Indeed I do and will continue it,...

Journal of Serjeant John Wilson, 15th Foot

Christian Davies, Royal Scots Greys, 1690s

Presumably she was brave, but she seems to have been a very coarse woman.

Richard Cannon, Historical Records of the Royal Regiments of Scots Dragoons

Christian Davies, also known as Mother Ross, a woman who served undetected as a trooper in the Scots Dragoons (later the Royal Scots Greys and now the Royal Scots Dragoon Guards) 1690s. NMS

A naval press gang, 1740s

As I crossed Tower Wharf, a squat tawny fellow, with a hanger by his side and a cudgel in his hand, came up to me, calling, 'Yo, Ho!, brother, you must come along with me'. As I did not like his appearance, I quickened my pace, in hope of ridding myself of his company; upon which he whistled aloud, and immediately another sailor appeared before me, who laid hold of me by the collar, and began to drag me along. Not being of a humour to relish such treatment, I disengaged myself of the assailant, and with one blow of my cudgel laid him motionless on the ground; and perceiving myself surrounded in a trice by ten or a dozen more, exerted myself with such dexterity and success that some of my opponents were fain to attack me with drawn cutlasses; and after an obstinate engagement, in which I received a large wound on my head, and another on my left cheek, I was disarmed, taken prisoner, and carried on board a pressing tender, where, after being pinioned like a malefactor, I was thrust down into the hold among a parcel of miserable wretches, the sight of whom well-nigh distracted me. As the commanding officer had not humanity enough to order my wounds to be dressed, and as I could not use my own hands, I desired one of my fellow-captives, who was

Pen and watercolour drawing of HMS Edinburgh, the third warship to bear that name, by A C Jeffreys, c1810-60. NMS

[28]

unfettered, to take a handkerchief out of my pocket and tie it round my head to stop the bleeding. He pulled out my handkerchief 'tis true; but instead of applying it to the use for which I had designed it, went to the grating of the hatchway, and with astonishing composure, sold it before my face to a bumboat woman then on board for a quart of gin, with which he treated my companions, regardless of my circumstances and entreaties. I complained bitterly of this robbery to the midshipman on deck, telling him that unless my hurts were dressed I should bleed to death. But compassion was a weakness of which no man could justly accuse this person, who, squirting a mouthful of dissolved tobacco upon me through the grating, told me, 'I was a mutinous dog, and that I might die and be damned'.

Tobias Smollett *Roderick Random*

An unknown sailor from Ness, World War I.
Scottish Life Archive

The Forfarshire Sodger

In Forfar I was born and bred,
And faith I do think shame, sir,
To tell the sober life I lived
Before I came from hame, sir.
Hurrah, hurrah, my tiddy alaira lido.

At school I learned to read and write
And count the rule o' three, sir,
When a nobler thought came into my head,
That a sodger I wad be, sir.
Hurrah, hurrah, my tiddy alaira lido.

As I gaed up through Forfar glen
And doon through Forfar county,
'Twas there I met with Sergeant Brown
For forty punds o' bounty.
Hurrah, hurrah, my tiddy alaira lido.

'Twas there I spent most of my time,
Marching up and doon, sir,
Wi' a feathered bonnet upon my head
And powdered to the croon, sir.
Hurrah, hurrah, my tiddy alaira lido.

But fegs they gart me change my tune,
And sent me aff to Spain, sir,
Where forty regiments all in a row
Came marchin' owre the plain, sir.
Hurrah, hurrah, my tiddy alaira lido.

'Twas three long days we fought wi' them,
The battle all in vain, sir,
When a bullet came whistlin' through my legs,
And I rose and fired again, sir.
Hurrah, hurrah, my tiddy alaira lido.

The doctor came and dressed my wounds,
And swore that I was lame, sir,
But I got haud o' twa shovel shafts,
And I cam' hirplin' hame, sir.
Hurrah, hurrah, my tiddy alaira lido.

The hardships that I hae come through,
I scarcely need to mention,
For noo I'm sittin' in the toon
And livin' on my pension.
Hurrah, hurrah, my tiddy alaira lido.

David Shaw (1786-1856)

The Dumfries Volunteers

Does haughty Gaul invasion threat,
Then let the louns bewaure, Sir,
There's wooden walls upon our seas,
And volunteers on shore, Sir:
The Nith shall run to Corsincon,
And Criffel sink in Solway,
Ere we permit a foreign foe
On British ground to rally.

O let us not, like snarling tykes,
In wrangling be divided,
Till, slap! come in an unco' loun,
And wi' a rung decide it!
Be Britain still to Britain true,
Amang oursels united;
For never but by British hands
Must British wrongs be righted.

The kettle o' the Kirk and State,
Perhaps a clout may fail in't,
But de'il a foreign tinkler loun
Shall ever ca' a nail in't:
Our fathers' blude the kettle bought,
And wha wad dare to spoil it,
By heavens! the sacrilegious dog
Shall fuel be to boil it!

Granatiere del XXV Reggimento con il suo = Abito di Uniforme.

A grenadier of the 25th Regiment of Foot in Minorca, about 1769. NMS

The wretch that would a tyrant own,
And th' wretch, his true-sworn brother,
Who'd set the mob above the throne,
May they be damned together!
Who will not sing, GOD SAVE THE KING.
Shall hang as high't the steeple;
But while we sing, GOD SAVE THE KING.
We'll ne'er forget THE PEOPLE.

Robert Burns (1759-96)

Print referring to the Duke of York's unsuccessful campaign in Flanders, 1793,
shows the Duke astride a cannon barrel with caricatures of different types of
soldier, including a Highlander and a black musician. NMS

The Athole Volunteers, late eighteenth century

An anecdote is told, which illustrates the manner in which some of these men were procured:- an Englishman in a journey through Athole, one morning, observed a poor fellow running to the hills as for his life, closely pursued by half a dozen human blood hounds. Turning to his guide, the gentleman anxiously inquired the meaning of what he saw. 'Ou,' replied the imperturbable Celt, 'it's only the Duke raising the royal Athole *volunteers.*'

G Penny *Traditions of Perth*

Twa recruitin' sergeants

Twa recruitin' sergeants frae the Black Watch,
Tae mercats and fairms some recruits fur tae catch,
But a that they 'listed was just ane or twa,
Enlist my bonnie laddie, and come awa.

For it is over the mountains, and over the main,
Through Gibraltar tae France and tae Spain
With a feather tae your bunnet and a kilt abune your knee,
Enlist my bonnie laddie, and come awa wi me.

Wi your tattie pu'in and your meal and your kale,
Your soor soor sowans and your ill-brewed ale,
Wi your buttermilk and whey and yer breid bak'd raw,
Enlist my bonnie laddie, and come awa.

Laddie, o ye dinna ken the danger that you're in,
If yer horse is with stiff legs or your rowsin was tae rin?
The greedy auld fairmer he widnae pey your fee,
Enlist my bonnie laddie, and come awa.

It's intae the barn and it's oot o the byre,
This auld fairmer thinks you'll never tire,
A slave for a life of low decree -
Enlist my bonnie laddie, and come awa.

Laddie, if you've got a sweetheart or a bairn,
You'll easily get rid o that ill-spun yarn,
Twa rattles on the drum and, aye, that will pey for a,
Enlist my bonnie laddie, and come awa.

Traditional

Recruiting bill for the 71st (Fraser's) Highlanders, 1776. NMS

Volunteers Wanted,

For General FRASER's Highland Regiment, to consist of two Battalions, the greatest part of which are already raised.

THis is to give notice to all gentlemen Volunteers, who are able and willing to serve his Majesty *King George*, that *Ensign Thomas Hamilton*, in said regiment, has opened a rendezvous at *Dundee*, (at Mrs Carmichael's), *Perth, Dunkeld*, and *Pittenweem*, where Volunteers will be immediately received. His stay will be short in this country, as he goes south in March next, to deliver over his men to the regiment. Persons, therefore, willing to enter into this regiment, (which holds forth such lucrative terms) will do well not to miss this opportunity. *No price will be grudged* for good men, who will (besides the bounty-money) enter into present pay and good quarters. The advantages that will arise to those who inlist into this *corps*, are very great. They are to go to *America*, and by his *Majesty's royal* and *most gracious proclamation*, they will be intitled to a *full discharge* at the end of *three years, that is in* 1779, or of the present *American rebellion*. Now, considering that the British army will be from forty to fifty thousand men strong, there, in spring next, it cannot, in all human probability, fail to be entirely quelled, next summer. Then, *gentlemen*, will be your *harvest*, and the best one too you ever *cropt*. You will, each of you, by visiting this *new world*, become the *founders of families*. The lands of the *rebels* will be divided amongst you, and every one of you become *lairds*. No old regiment will have such advantages. Is not this better than starving at home in these poor times? and will a man of spirit sit unmoved, and hear such proffered terms? Ye who are now dreading the sentence of *stool-meal*, who are drudging like slaves under a *cruel* or *harsh task-master*. Any of you who have got a *termagant* or *cross wife*, or who smart under the displeasure of an *ungracious parent*, come all to *Ensign Thomas Hamilton*, and he will ease your fears, and make you at once free and happy.

Dundee, Jan. 8. 1776.   *GOD save the KING.*

A Birmingham boy enlists in a Highland regiment

In September, 1891, a very ordinary family of twelve were sitting round the dinner table - Father, Mother and ten children, when I casually mentioned to one of my brothers that my friend intended joining the Seaforth Highlanders and that I should like to go with him.

At this announcement there was a silence for a few moments, then one of my sisters said, 'Huh! You would be too afraid to go for a soldier.'

Although only sixteen years of age I said to myself, 'I'll show them whether I am afraid or not.' So I went with my young friend the next day and saw the Recruiting Sergeant. After looking me over, he said, 'Don't forget to say you are eighteen, or you won't pass through.'

French print depicting a Highland soldier with his family in Paris, 1815. Wives and children sometimes accompanied soldiers on campaign.
NMS

... It was a sad leaving, as I had never left home before, although one of a family of twelve. But I soon brightened up, as the next day we were sent to Fort George, our Regimental Depot in the north of Scotland, about seven miles from Inverness, and fitted out with our gorgeous Highland uniform, with kilt, sporran, feather hat and red tunic, etc., which I really think was the attraction to boys of our age at the time. How proud we were the first time we were allowed out 'on pass'.

A F Corbett *Service through six reigns: 1891 to 1953*

The ideal NCO, 90th Light Infantry, 1848

SECTION XIII. NON-COMMISSIONED OFFICER

1. A Non-commissioned Officer will always be prompt and decisive, though temperate, towards the men, on all occasions; and when he has to order a man into confinement in a state of drunkenness, he will have him confined at once, taking care not to touch him himself, always remembering that it is idle to reason with a drunken man, and cruel to irritate him.

Regimental standing orders, 90th Light Infantry

In Memoriam Private D Sutherland

Killed in action in the German trench 16 May 1916,
and the others who died

So you were David's father,
And he was your only son,
And the new-cut peats are rotting
And the work is left undone,
Because of an old man weeping,
Just an old man in pain,
For David, his son David,
That will not come again.
Oh, the letters he wrote you
And I can see them still,
Not a word of the fighting
But just the sheep on the hill
And how you should get the crops in
Ere the year got stormier,
And the Bosches have got his body,
And I was his officer.
You were only David's father,
But I had fifty sons
When we went up in the evening
Under the arch of the guns,

And we came back at twilight -
O God! I heard them call
To me for help and pity
That could not help at all.
Oh, never will I forget you,
My men that trusted me,
More my sons than your fathers',
For they could only see
The little helpless babies
And the young men in their pride.
They could not see you dying,
And hold you while you died.
Happy and young and gallant,
They saw their first-born go,
But not the strong limbs broken
And the beautiful men brought low,
The piteous writhing bodies,
They screamed, 'Don't leave me, sir,'
For they were only your fathers
But I was your officer.

Ewart Alan Mackintosh

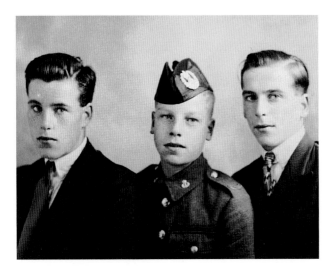

*Home on leave in
1936, boy soldier
David McCorry of
the Cameron
Highlanders went
into Edinburgh to
have his photograph
taken at Jerome's
with his brothers,
Charlie and Dick.*
Mrs B McCorry

A conscientious objector surprises a relation, World War I

My father had a distant relative living in Leeds, which is not far from Wakefield. He wrote him and said his son was a CO in Wakefield and he suggested that the relative might invite me to come to tea some time. He knew the spartan conditions in which I was living. When I got the invitation I set out. I was able to go into Wakefield by bus - one of the rules was that we were not to go anywhere by train. This was to prevent our going home to see our wives or parents at the weekends.

When my relative came to his door in Leeds he couldn't believe his eyes. He had understood from the abbreviation CO that I was a Commanding Officer. The figure before him was wearing a very shabby Home Office suit. I had to break the news to him of my far from glamorous situation, but he gave me my tea all right and treated me civilly.

J P M Millar, in Ian MacDougall *Voices from war*

A child's view, World War I

My father was called up when conscription came in and he was called to appear before a tribunal. An army captain presided who was really vicious in his hatred. All the details were in the papers. I was sent actually to relatives, in order to spare me this experience.

My father's conscientious objection was on religious grounds. Well, he didn't want to take life. He believed that it was wrong to kill and take life and he refused to do so, because in the Bible it is said you must not kill. And Jesus said that if his Father had wanted him to do anything like that... Anyway my father wanted to obey God rather than men. And he stood firm on that.

At that time my father was employed with a big firm and his boss was furious because he was a very patriotic man. All the staff who joined the Forces were given a certain amount of their salary to be retained for them. But not so my father.

He was told by the tribunal that he had to find work of national importance, because he wasn't to be sent to prison. So he contacted a firm where he had worked as a young man as an engineer. He had had to give this up because he had had a very serious illness at one time and was quite ill for a long time. However, the firm were very pleased to hear from him again and they said they would be delighted to have him work with them. He went to Kirkcaldy from Perth, where we lived, to work. So he worked there for quite

AUCHTERMUCHTY PARISH CHURCH
JUNIOR CHOIR—WAR CONCERT, 1915.
"KNITTING SONG"

a long time and his salary at that was £5 a week, which had to cover his board and lodging and keep us at home. So you can imagine we had quite a hard time.

I was at the secondary school, Perth Academy, at the time. When I went back to school after this happened it was just like being sent to Coventry. The pupils just ignored me, except for one or two of my own special friends. The teachers didn't ignore me. The teachers didn't even mention it. It was just the pupils, which rather surprised me but I realised than that their parents must have read the newspapers.

I can't remember my mother being taunted as a result of my father being a conscientious objector, I can't remember that at all. I think the neighbours were all very pleasant to her. I can't remember my mother being taunted in any way by anyone.

Dorothy Wiltshire, in Ian MacDougall *Voices from war*

The Junior Choir of Auchtermuchty Parish Church sang while they knitted woollen garments for soldiers at the front, World War I. Scottish Life Archive

Battalion shooting team, 1st Volunteer Battalion (Inverness Highland) The Queen's Own Cameron Highlanders, Inverness, 1887. NMS

The kilt versus trews again, circa 1931

When I sat for the final exams I discovered with pleasure mixed with surprise that they came quite easily to me and as I had also accumulated a very nice bonus of marks for being an Under-officer, my entry into the Argylls seemed purely a formality. Everything in the garden was beautiful - a fatal situation for me.

Just before the end of term, all cadets who were graduating were given a War Office form to fill in: 'Name in order of preference three regiments into which you desire to be commissioned.' I wrote as follows:

1. The Argyll and Sutherland Highlanders
2. The Black Watch

and then for some reason which I never fully understood, possibly because it was the only one of the six Highland Regiments that wore trews instead of the kilt, I wrote,

3. Anything but the Highland Light Infantry.

Somebody at the War Office was funnier than I was and I was promptly commissioned into the Highland Light Infantry.

David Niven *The moon's a balloon*

Ramsay MacDonald at Invergordon, 1931

Len Johnson, a stoker, claims to have a clear recollection of the Prime Minister's visit.

The skipper cleared lower deck. The whole crew was assembled in the hangar. All planes were put up on the flight decks, giving us space. When we'd all assembled inside the hangar the Captain introduced Ramsay MacDonald and his retinue, who stood on a dais. Ramsay MacDonald spoke to us, then the Captain, in the usual tradition, called for three hearty cheers for Ramsay MacDonald. We were so damned incensed that we'd have blown Ramsay MacDonald through a torpedo tube.

So the Captain gets his hat in the traditional way, waves it round, 'Hip! Hip!... They all of them went R-R-R-R-P! One bloody great raspberry!

Of course the Captain's face was as red as a beetroot, so was Ramsay's and everybody else. So he had another go. Round again. 'Hip! Hip!...' 'R-R-R-R-P!' Again. Because you always give three anyway. Round he goes again, and he got the biggest result of all time...

At this point my skills in transliteration fail; I cannot adequately convey the vigour with which an old sailor can illustrate a thousand men blowing the biggest raspberry in the world.

Alan Ereira *The Invergordon mutiny*

These figures on an anti-Fascist float in the May Day parade, Glasgow, 1938, represent Adolf Hitler, Neville Chamberlain and Benito Mussolini.
Scottish Life Archive

Evacuation, 1 September 1939

On Friday, 1st September 1939, evacuation began... The results of planning and rehearsals became apparent. Steadily and methodically parents and children made their way to the appointed classrooms or to the defined positions in the playground. A registration department had to be improvised, for up to the last minute in flocked parents who had changed their minds and decided to be evacuated. Helpers from voluntary societies and Corporation offices arrived, eagerly inquiring where they were to go and what they were to do. By 7a.m. curious spectators, congregated outside the playground, greeted the panting late-comers with unappreciated witticisms. In classrooms mothers awkwardly fitting themselves into small desks renewed acquaintance with the place where as children they had learned their lessons. After unavailing efforts to keep the whole family perched on the neighbouring desks, an exasperated mother's admonition of 'Ah'll sort you!' was followed by the belated commiseration, 'My! Teacher, I dinna ken how you get on wi' forty or fifty weans a' the time!' Whereupon other mothers joined in the conversation, and teacher and parents found a common bond of friendship. Registers were marked, with frequent amendments for late-comers. Identity labels were attached round the necks of evacuees, and the names of owners were placed on an assortment of light luggage. Suitcases, attaché cases, pillowslips, haversacks and parcels of every shape and size had to be securely fastened and labelled. As time sped, responsibility upon the head master increased. Some children were clearly without a sufficiency of clothing; were they to be allowed to go? Those who resided nearby were sent home in a last effort to obtain additional personal wear. Orders were given however, that every child present, unless suffering from an infectious disease, was to be evacuated. Worse still, many of the children had been away from school on holiday and, as a result, had not been medically inspected for weeks or months. Teachers knew what might be the condition of some children, but little could be done at such short notice... .

Two abreast the evacuees made their way along the streets. Songs quickened the pace. Wishes of good luck from spectators at windows were answered with ringing cheers. For most of the children evacuation was something in the nature of an adventure. Too young to realise the significance of their departure from home, they marched in buoyant spirits. The only worried people were the mothers and fathers.

William Boyd Bickley (ed) *Evacuation in Scotland*

Joining the Royal Air Force, 1939

I don't think there wis any specific reason I went to the Air Force rather then the army or the navy, except the Air Force was needin' people and we thought we'd mair chance o' getting away. I think that was mair the reason we volunteered: we didnae want tae go in the army. God Almighty! Just imagine yourself rushin' across a battlefield wi' a bayonet and a big six foot man comin' rushin' at ye! Ah'd ha' died o fright! Up in the air everybody's the same size.

Bill King, in Ian MacDougall *Voices from war*

Pilots of the Royal Flying Corps, World War I. NMS

Brigadier Sir Bernard and the Australians, World War II

My father used to tell the following story about Brigadier Sir Bernard Fergusson.

Sir Bernard was commanding a force which included some Australian troops. On the first day he appeared before them, as usual wearing his monocle, and inspected them. On the next occasion that they met, every one of the Australians standing before him had the metal 'crown' cap of a beer bottle screwed into the same eye. Sir Bernard looked at them levelly. He then removed the monocle from his eye, threw it in the air, and expertly caught it again in his eye socket. 'Now, do that,' he said.

Needless to say, he won the instant approval of the Australian troops.

The Editor

Lieutenant Primrose, Burma-Siam railway, World War II

One of the guards told us one day that the previous occupant of our cell had been a POW, a Scotsman named Primrose. He described his uniform as though it had a skirt, and said that he had been charged with the murder of a fellow-prisoner. We were deeply curious about this Scottish soldier in his kilt and probed our guard as much as we dared. The story that came out was one of those legends that later circulated around the network of prisons and camps, a rumour so strange it could be true. Primrose was a lieutenant in the Argyll and Sutherland Highlanders, and in the middle of 1943 had been in a

Officers of 51st (Highland) Division captured in 1940, who were prisoners of war in Oflag VII B, Eichstett, Germany, formed a Pipe Band. NMS

camp far up the railway. The Japanese sent in a huge labour force of Tamils, who were as usual treated like atomized slaves, starved and brutalized and dying in handfuls every week. Cholera broke out in the Tamil camp, and the Japanese railway administration found a novel way of containing the epidemic: they shot its victims.

When a single British POW caught the disease he was moved to an isolation tent on the outskirts of the camp, to await 'disposal'. Primrose happened by the tent in time to see two Japanese guards carry the feverish soldier out to a tree. One of them prepared to shoot him, from a considerable distance; the guard was clearly nervous and incompetent, and would almost certainly only wound the prisoner, prolonging his agony needlessly. Primrose grabbed his rifle and shot the man himself with a single round to his heart. And for this he was charged with murder.

I wondered what had happened to him: had they already killed him for his act of loving violence? For years I remained fascinated by what Primrose had done, his decisiveness and compassion. It seemed so symbolic of what they had reduced us to, that he should have to kill one of his own men out of kindness.

[After the Liberation]... As we restored our contact with the army and the world we began to find endings for some of the stories we'd had to tell each other over and over, never certain of their proper outcome, for the past three years. The Australian nurses at Banka Island, for example: fifty of them had died, even more than we thought, but two of them had survived. Primrose, the humane murderer of his own soldier, was not executed but returned to the railway, and he had survived.

Eric Lomax The railway man

Arriving for Commando training, Achnacarry, 1942

Seven miles - in this rain! There was a lot of moaning and groaning as we formed up. Then, headed and flanked by instructors, off we went. The piper was playing a tune that would have made the dead get up and march - which, in our case, was almost essential. The instructors looked as if they were out to enjoy a short stroll. We - as someone muttered at the time - looked as if we were about to march seven bloody miles through the bloody rain...

We were halted just inside the main gate. Somehow or other, I summoned up the strength to raise my head and look around me. Everywhere I looked, soldiers were on the move. Some were doubling here and there in squads, N.C.O.s barking at them like collies chasing on sheep. Others were drilling under Guards sergeants - easily recognised by their pace sticks, and their voices. Outside the camp, more men were crawling up an almost perpendicular rock face like khaki flies.

Then I saw the graves. There was a long row of them alongside the trees that lined the driveway. They were marked by white crosses. Nailed to each cross was a small board bearing a number, rank, and name, under which was given the cause of death. I could read the two nearest me.

'He showed himself on the skyline.'

'He failed to take cover in an assault landing.'

I felt like chuckling, but somehow couldn't quite make it. The graves were phoney, of course... Or, were they?

Evidently the others had noticed the graves too. And at least one man shared my misgivings. He gestured at the row of crosses and said to an instructor: 'Come off it. Who do you think you're kidding?'

Donald Gilchrist *Castle Commando*

A conscientious objector, Edinburgh, World War II

Anyway a big shot - the Commanding Officer in the Castle - came round to inspect us in the guardhouse. Everybody had their beds tidy and their boots in the proper place. I'd just made up mine as if I were at home. In he came. We were all shouted at to 'Stand to attention!' They all sprang to attention. And I didn't. I was sitting on the edge of my bed and I just stayed sitting. I didn't get up. And the Commanding Officer flushed crimson and started shouting and bawling at me. I said, 'You don't realise I'm not in the army. I'm a pacifist. They've summoned me to the army but I'm not going because I'm a pacifist. I've resigned.' He nearly exploded. I thought he was going to burst. But I didn't get up on my feet. The rest of the soldiers hearing a major general or whatever he was being talked to like that, sitting on the end of my bed, 'Oh, no, I'm not standing up. I'm not in the army' - wonderful! So what they thought of me in that tough place suddenly rose. I was their lily-white boy after that.

... Let me say a little about the response to us conshies in the Non-Combatant Corps by the Regular army or air force people. Near Aldershot, when we were stationed there, we were continually meeting Grenadier Guards, Scots Guards, Irish Guards, meeting them at dances, and especially coming home on leave, the compartment filled with other soldiers. Not once did any of them abuse us, not once. I remember coming up home to

Edinburgh once on leave on the train. Seven other regular army chaps were in the compartment: four soldiers on that side, three on this, as well as me. Of course, I was wearing my uniform with NCC on the badge. One of the soldiers said, 'What does NCC stand for? Norwegian Camel Corps?' I said, 'No. We're conscientious objectors.' And there was quite a bit of talk about that. There were two ways of looking at it. One was, 'Oh, I'd have done that but I'm not clever enough.' I said, 'It's nothing to do with cleverness.' So - 'Oh, no, no, they'd just twist me round their fingers.' And the other attitude was, 'Well, I'd have done it but I wasn't brave enough.' As if it was brave being a conchie. But never a word of abuse from the armed forces - just the civilians. Oh, the civilians were different. When we were marching through the streets in Liverpool on our way to the docks, where we were fire-watching, quite often the general public would shout things at us. 'Yellowbelly!' was the favourite one. But never from the armed forces.

Norman MacCaig, in Ian MacDougall *Voices from war*

ONE SOLDIER, ONE SAUSAGE

Daily life in the forces and at home

A Scottish naval surgeon observes the effects of oranges upon scurvy, 1747

Oil painting by P J de Loutherbourg of the Battle of Camperdown, 11 October 1797: the hero of the day was Admiral Duncan, later Viscount Duncan of Camperdown. NMS

On the 27th of May, I took twelve patients in the scurvy on board the *Salisbury* at sea. Their cases were as similar as I could have them. They all in general had putrid gums, the spots and lassitude, with weakness of their knees. They lay together in one place, being a proper apartment for the sick in the fore-hold; and had one diet common to all, viz., water gruel sweetened with sugar in the morning; fresh mutton broth often times for dinner; at other times puddings, boiled biscuit with sugar etc.; and for supper barley, raisins, rice and currants, sago and wine, or the like. Two of these were ordered each a quart of cyder a day. Two others took twenty five gutts of elixir vitriol three times a day upon an empty stomach, using a gargle strongly acidulated with it for their mouths. Two others took two spoonfuls of

vinegar three times a day upon an empty stomach, having their gruels and their other food well acidulated with it, as also the gargles for the mouth. Two of the worst patients, with the tendons in the ham rigid (a symptom none of the rest had) were put under a course of sea water. Of this they drank half a pint every day and sometimes more or less as it operated by way of gentle physic. Two others had each two oranges and one lemon given them every day. These they eat with greediness at different times upon an empty stomach. They continued but six days under this course, having consumed the quantity that could be spared. The two remaining patients took the bigness of a nutmeg three times a day of an electuary recommended by an hospital surgeon made of garlic, mustard seed, *rad. raphan.*, balsam of peru and gum myrrh, using for common drink barley water well acidulated with tamarinds, by a decoction of which, with the addition of *cremor tartar*, they were gently purged three or four times during the course.

This exquisite miniature of an unknown officer in the Argyllshire Fencibles was painted by G Englehart, c1795

The consequence was that the most sudden and visible good effects were perceived from the use of the oranges and lemons; one of those who had taken them being at the end of six days fit for duty. The spots were not indeed at that time quite off his body, nor his gums sound; but without any other medicine than a gargarism of elixir of vitriol he became quite healthy before we came into Plymouth, which was on the 16th June. The other was the best recovered of any in his condition, and being now deemed pretty well was appointed to nurse the rest of the sick.

James Lind *A treatise of the scurvy*

Flogging in Perth, circa 1776

After the Athole Highlanders, the 2nd battalion of the Black Watch were filled up at Perth; and the Macdonald Highlanders, a fine body of newly raised men, 1000 strong, were trained here. They were succeeded by a body of Irish troops, called the White Boys, from being dressed in white jackets...

There being no barracks, the soldiers were all billeted on the inhabitants, and in most cases were wretchedly lodged; often in open tiled garrets with an unglazed window, or in dismal vaults fit only for pigs. - Incredible as it may now appear, this regiment, when in Perth, were under stoppages, which left the men only 3d a day. Their common breakfast was a half-penny roll, and a half-penny worth of Suffolk cheese; and those who sought to alleviate their sufferings by taking a glass of spirits, got no more food for twenty-four hours. The consequence was, that these men, from sheer necessity, were frequently driven to commit petty depredations, and as these, when discovered, were followed by punishments quite disproportionate to the offence, the North Inch became a scene of continual barbarity. It was no uncommon thing to see six, or even ten, of these unfortunate wretches suffer from 100 to 500 lashes each; and this was continued day after day, till sometimes the washerwomen interfered, and, partly by threats and partly by entreaty, succeeded in getting a few of them pardoned. At length a circumstance occurred which put an end to these *public* inhuman and disgusting

Captain Sir William Kerr arrives back late at General Lord Moira's house in Queen Street, Edinburgh, to find the General waiting up for him, July 1804. NMS

exhibitions. A fine looking man, who had a wife and four children, driven by absolute want, entered a potato field in the vicinity, and pulled up a couple of shaws; nine potatoes were said to be the whole amount. Being detected in the act, he was complained of to the commanding officer, tried by court martial, and sentenced to receive 500 lashes. He was brought out to the Inch for punishment; but the peculiar circumstances of the case had created unusual sympathy in his behalf, and brought out a vast number of the inhabitants. On the way thither, the commanding officer was met by the wife, with an infant at her breast, and three at her side. She entreated him to have mercy on her husband; but he turned from her with contempt. She seized him by the sleeve, and implored, with tears in her eyes - but in vain; he thrust her from him with violence. These circumstances were soon communicated by those who had witnessed the interview, which inflamed the minds of the people even more against the commander... The moment the prisoner was untied from the halberts, a general attack was made upon the officers. The adjutant was less fortunate than some of the others in escaping. He got a terrible mauling from the women; who laid him down on his belly, in which position he was held by some scores of vigorous hands, till he got a handsome flogging on the bare posteriors, in the presence of thousands - inflicted with an energy that would remain inprinted on the memory till the day of his death.

G Penny *Traditions of Perth*

A tender mother, 1784

Mrs Baird of Newbyth, the mother of our distinguished countryman, the late General Sir David Baird, was always spoken of as a grand specimen of the class. When the news arrived from India of the gallant but unfortunate action of '84 against Hyder Ali, in which her son, then Captain Baird, was engaged, it was stated that he and other officers had been taken prisoners and chained together two and two. The friends were careful in breaking such sad intelligence to the mother of Captain Baird. When, however, she was made fully to understand the position of her son and his gallant companions, disdaining all weak and useless expressions of her own grief, and knowing well the restless and athletic habits of her son, all she said was, 'Lord pity the chiel that's chained to oor Davie.'

Dean Ramsay *Reminiscences of Scottish life and character*

The landlord's advice, an optimistic view. A naive watercolour of two Scottish soldiers drinking: they wear
the uniforms of the 93rd Highlanders and Highland Borderers Militia (90th). NMS

Food and home comforts in Ceylon, 1803

At night we got what was called supper, which consisted of a small cake of rice flour and water, and a liquid called coffee, although there was not a single grain of the berry in it. What we used for sugar was called jaggery, which was made up in cakes, very insipid and dirty; it bore no resemblance to the sugar used in Europe. At eight o'clock in the morning we got breakfast brought to us in the same manner; it consisted of the same cake, fish, or bullocks' liver, and jaggery water, and this formed the daily diet of the British troops in Ceylon. Had it been of good quality, and properly cooked, it was well enough, our allowance of liquor, which was arrack, was one quart per day to five men, or about two drams to each.

The beef, of which we had a pound per day, was given out along with the rice in the morning, for which sixpence per day was kept off our pay. But it was rather carrion than beef. The cattle sometimes buffaloes, sometimes bullock, having been used in their husbandry were generally lean, old or diseased, the meat was soft, flabby, and full of membraneous skin; it had a rank, heavy, loathsome odour, was offensive to both sight and smell, and hurt me more than the climate, and was, I am certain, the cause of much of the disease and death which thinned our numbers. The rice, too, was small, and of a bad quality, full of dust and dirt, from which our rascally cooks were at no trouble to free it.

Alexander Alexander *The life of Alexander Alexander*

It tak's a deal o' dirt to poison sogers, Edinburgh, 1804

Loose and noisy as this lodging was, we were well enough satisfied with it for our quarters; and our landlady, who was the wife of some veteran serving abroad, knew well how to manage her house so as to make the most of it.

I shall mention here our usual meals (with which we were perfectly contented) during the time we were in quarters, as they differ so widely from what soldiers now-a-days are accustomed to; premising, that we had our provisions, without contract, at our own purchasing. We breakfasted about nine in the morning, on bread and milk; dined about two in the afternoon, on potatoes and a couple of salt herrings, boiled in the pot with the potatoes: a bottle of small beer (commonly called swipes) and a slice of bread served for supper, when we were disposed to take that meal, which soldiers seldom do. On the whole, I am certain our expenses for messing, dear as markets were, did not exceed three shillings and sixpence each, weekly; and to do our landlady justice, she was not anxious to encourage extravagance in preparing and cooking our meals, particularly as required fuel and attention; and, in these matters, we were far from being troublesome or particular. Our obliging landlady would, when requested, bring us a pennyworth of soup, called *kale*, for our dinner, instead of herring; and, if we had a little cause to remark on the want of cleanliness in the dish, or its contents, she jocosely replied, 'It tak's a deal o' dirt to poison sogers.'

James Anton *Retrospect of a military life*

Abandoned in Edinburgh, 1804

In a small closet adjoining that which we were to occupy, lodged three unfortunate girls, lately arrived from Hamilton, from which place they had been induced (by promises of marriage) to follow their lovers, now stationed near Edinburgh. These poor girls, after being drawn so far from home, were disappointed, and they now felt ashamed to return. Yet, although they had acted so inconsiderately, and perhaps with some levity, they were neither idly nor wantonly inclined; they were diligently employed a few days tambouring fine muslin, and when this work failed, they rose early every morning, walked barefooted to Leith, and were there employed unshipping coals. At night they returned to a cold welcomeless house, to prepare their scanty meal; while some ungenerous hints were thrown out, as they were turned from the fire, that they might not only keep the house in fuel, but themselves were above working at such a dirty job. These poor girls were sensible that they had acted wrong in leaving their home, relying on the faith of worthless lovers; but they were still honest, and as yet they had not been under the necessity of throwing themselves upon the town; and the only reply given to their jeering scoffers was a sigh or a tear. They removed from that loose lodging-house, but, left to their own exertions, and more exposed to ill-advisers and bad example, than to generous protectors, or good company, they fell victims to their own easy belief in the word of a lover.

James Anton *Retrospect of a military life*

An Artillery man's native wife, Ceylon, 1805

I then began to look for a wife, or rather a nurse - love was out of the question. My affections were elsewhere all engrossed; but I must either take a wife or die.

My choice fell upon a Cingalese; she was of a clear bronze colour, smooth-skinned, healthy and very cleanly in her person and manner of cooking, which was her chief recommendation. Puncheh was of a good or bad temper just as she had any object to gain, for ever crying out poverty, and always in want either of money or clothes. She imagined every person better off than herself; often pretended to be under the necessity to pawn her necklace and other ornaments, and boasted how much she was reduced since she came to live with me. Then she would pretend to be sick, and lie in bed for twenty-four hours together; and neither speak, nor take food or medicine, but lie and sulk. I was completely sick of her at times, for she would not leave me, neither would she stay.

When these sullen fits came on, I in vain endeavoured to sooth or flatter her; I had not money to satisfy her extravagance, my victuals remained uncooked, and the hut in confusion. There was no alternative but to follow the example of the others. I applied the strap of my great coat, which never failed to effect a cure, and all went on well for a time. She bore me a son, a fine little boy, who died young. Often have I sat and looked with delight upon his infant gambols. As is the custom here, he smoked cigars as soon as he could walk about. It was strange to see the infant puffing the smoke into the air, and forming circles with it, until weary, then running and placing his head upon his mother's bosom, to quench his thirst from her breast, before finishing his cigar.

Alexander Alexander *The life of Alexander Alexander*

The 71st smell Spanish sausages, 1808

When we were once housed, the Spaniards were very liberal in their *offers* of meat, but it was evidently with the expectation of our refusal; their oil and garlic being still detestable to us. Their fire-places were generally hung round with fine sausages, of which, I believe, it would not have required great eloquence to make us accept; but we seldom or never got the offer, I presume for this very reason. The wary people invariably sat up all night when we were in their houses, and watched us, as we lay on the floor, with the eyes of lynxes: they had, indeed, for some reason, as several attempts were made to pilfer their sausages; but in this we were seldom successful, a little salt being in general the amount of our thefts. That article hung in a box near the fire-place, exactly similar to what is usual in the common houses of Scotland.

Vicissitudes in the life of a Scottish soldier

The Walcheren expedition, 1809

At this time I got a distaste I could never overcome. A few of us went into a wine-store where there was a large tun with a ladder to get to the top, in which was a hole two feet square. There was not much wine in it, so we buckled our canteen straps together, until a camp-kettle attached to them reached the liquor. We drew it up once - we all drank; down it went again - it got entangled with something at the bottom of the tun - a candle was lowered; to our great disappointment, the corpse of a French soldier lay upon the bottom! Sickness came upon me, and for a long time afterwards, I shuddered at the sight of red wine.

Journal of a soldier of the 71st regiment

William Chambers remembers the prisoners of war at Penicuik, circa 1810

Here on a level space in the depth of a valley, was a group of barracks, surrounded by tall palisades, for the accommodation of some hundreds of prisoners, who, night and day, were strictly watched by armed sentries, ready to fire on them in the event of an outbreak. The day on which we happened to make our visit was a Sunday, and the scene presented was accordingly the more startling. Standing in the churchyard on the brink of the hollow, all the immediate surroundings betokened the solemnity of a Scottish Sabbath. The shops in the village were shut. From the church was heard the voice of the preacher. Looking down from the height on the hive of living beings, there was not among them a vestige of the ordinary calm of a Sunday - only Dimanche! Dressed in coarse woollen clothing of a yellow colour, and most of them wearing red or blue cloth caps, or partly-coloured cowls, the prisoners were engaged in a variety of amusements and occupations. Prominently, and forming the centre of attraction, were a considerable number ranked up in two rows, joyously dancing to the sound of a fiddle, which was briskly played by a man who stood on the top of a barrel. Others were superintending cookery in big pots over open fires, which they fanned by the flapping of cocked hats. Others were fencing with sticks amidst a circle of eager onlookers. A few men were seated meditatively on benches, perhaps thinking of far-distant homes, or the fortune of war, which had brought them into this painful predicament. In twos or threes, some were walking apart to and fro, and I conjectured they were of a slightly superior class. Near one corner was a booth - a rickety concern of boards - seemingly a kind of restaurant, with the pretentious inscription, 'CAFE DE PARIS', over the door, and a small tricolor flag was fluttering from a slender pole on the

roof. To complete the picture, fancy several of the prisoners, no doubt the more ingenious among them, stationed at small wickets opening with hinges in the tall palisades, offering for sale articles, such as snuff-boxes of bone, that they had been allowed to manufacture, and the money got by which sales procured them a few luxuries.

William Chambers *Chambers' journal*

E   Ecossais

Stunned and slightly singed, Colombo, 1811

One occurrence I witnessed here almost incredible: a Portuguese governor touched at Colombo, early in the year 1811; on the firing of the salute, Gunner Richard Clark was blown from the mouth of his gun right into the air, and alighted upon a rock at a considerable distance in the harbour, yet escaped without a bone being broken, almost unhurt. It was the most miraculous escape I ever witnessed; he was but an awkward soldier at the best; the gun of which he was No 1, went off by accident, but not just at the time of loading, otherwise the left arm, or perhaps both arms, of No 2 had been blown off, as No 2 loads and rams home, along with No 1. The gun was just loaded when she went off, through the negligence of Clark, in not spunging properly. He was not at his proper distance, like the other man, nor yet near enough to receive the whole flash. To the astonishment of everyone, he was seen in the air, the spunge-staff grasped in his right hand, the rammerhead downwards, which first struck the rock as he alighted on his breech. The rock was very thickly covered with sea weed. A party was sent down to bring up the body, as all concluded him killed upon the spot; he was brought up only stunned and slightly singed, and was at his duty again in a few days; while No. 5, who served the vent, had his thumb, with which the motion-hole is stopped during the loading, so severely burned, it was feared he must have lost it, and it was only saved by the skill of the surgeon.

Alexander Alexander *The life of Alexander Alexander*

French prisoners of war and local girls, 1814

A young woman ... was in a certain condition, one of the prisoners being said to be the father. She was advised by her friends to put the blame on a local man, but she declared: 'What wad I say when the bairn began to speak?'

J L Black *Penicuik and neighbourhood*

An exhilarating breakfast, Spain, 1813 or 1814

We had therefore to depend upon our daily allowance of provisions, which was limited to one pound of ship-biscuit, one pound of beef, and one-third of a pint of spirits. We received occasionally a little rice; but this was a gratuity to which we had no just claim, consequently not regularly issued. Had these articles been good, the quantity might have been sufficient, but the biscuit was frequently crushed to crumbs, or mouldered to dust, and the beef would not have been allowed a stall in the poorest market of Great Britain. The spirits were generally good, and, when mixed with a little biscuit, proved an exhilarating breakfast.

James Anton *Retrospect of a military life*

A trooper's first roast beef, Royal Scots Greys in England, 1831

The village live-stock upon the commons - dogs, hogs and asses; and old horses, which had once been in military service, now capered when they heard the trumpets, as if young again; all were set astir by the marching of a regiment among them. The cows hobbled to the farthest side of the common, having no sympathy for bright scarlet, or kettle drums. And the geese, which had survived the killing and the roasting at Christmas sheered off, and faced round at a distance to hiss us, as if they were disloyal geese, hissing a regiment of royal dragoons, or as if they knew that we, being Scotch dragoons, were ignorant of roast goose.

The dinners provided for us each day at the inns or public houses on which we were billeted, so different in quality and style of cooking from the dinners to which I had been accustomed, were also matters to be remembered. I had tasted roast mutton at the winter suppers at Branxton, the annual festivals after harvest, but never at home. At Horsham, which was our first day's destination, we had roast beef and apple puddings for dinner at the house where I was quartered; the first roast beef which I had tasted during my life, and the first apple puddings which I had any recollections of. At Guildford, Chertsey, and Windsor, the fare was English, but I do not remember if it was entirely new to me. At Thame, in Oxfordshire, where we staid on the Saturday night, the Sunday, and the Sunday night, I was billetted on a house where we had roast goose for dinner on the Sunday - that was my first introduction to roast goose. Bicester, Banbury, and Warwick, were our next quarters. At Warwick I was made acquainted, for the first time, with Yorkshire pudding.

... If you listen to soldiers who have frequently marched in England, Scotland and Ireland, you will hear the Englishman calling Scotland any-

Cooks of the 1st Battalion the Cameronians (Scottish Rifles) at Aldershot, 1883. Clues to their trade can be seen in the cleaver held by the man seated second from right, and the rabbit dangling at extreme right. NMS

thing but a respectable portion of Her Majesty's dominions. Scotchmen are not satisfied to hear their country miscalled, but they are obliged to shake their heads and admit that there is no dinner for them, when marching there, as in England. They rally for Scotland, however, and remind the Englishman of the whisky, how plentiful that was.

Alexander Somerville, *Autobiography of a working man*

The 45th taste shark, 1837

On November 12, 1837, the skeleton of the 45th embarked at Madras for home, and we had among us a good many who had been away for nineteen years, and looked forward with mixed feelings to their return and the inevitable changes that must await them. Safe on board, we were off. We touched at Cape Town, and remained two days taking in water and supplies. A few bags of potatoes were given us, which were deemed a great luxury; and one of the sailors caught a shark, part of which I ate with great relish, for anything fresh is always first-class at sea, however it might taste on shore.

John Menzies, *Reminiscences of an old soldier*

A theological opinion, Royal Scots Greys, 1841

Those who knew him [the hospital sergeant] best alleged that there were only two other men in the regiment as disagreeable as he, one of them a Highlandman from Lochaber. I was one of nine men in the same barrack room with him. He was a genius for the invention of misery. The regimental tailor, after much theological and philosophical study, could only arrive at the opinion that this Highlandman had come out of Lochaber to trouble other men for their sins.

Alexander Somerville *Autobiography of a working man*

90th Light Infantry, 1848

SECTION XV: MARRIAGE

1. No woman is to be allowed to reside in Barracks who objects to make herself useful in Cooking, &c. It cannot be too often repeated to the men that they are on no account to marry without leave. A Man marrying, without having obtained leave from the Commanding Officer of the Regiment, will never be permitted to receive any of the indulgences bestowed on such as marry by consent. It is impossible to point out the inconveniences which arise and the evils which follow a Regiment encumbered with Women: poverty and misery are the inevitable consequences. Officers therefore cannot do too much to deter their men from marrying; and there are few men, however hard they may think it at the moment, that after a short period, will not be much obliged to them for having done so.

Regimental standing orders, 90th Light Infantry

Marriage without reflection, 1867

I think the women generally of that class in England look more to the future and hesitate to marry a soldier, whereas in Ireland, and indeed in Scotland, they do not think about it, they marry them at once without reflecting. I think that the young women in England are more careful about marrying a soldier.

Colonel Collingwood Dickson, to the
Royal Commission on Recruiting for the Army

Stony diet, South Africa, 1900

Well! we were on another forced march again, sometimes on half rations, and sometimes on quarter rations, and sometimes no drinking water available. Many a mile have I trudged along with a small stone in my mouth, the streams and wells being poisoned by the carcasses of dead horses and cattle having been thrown there by the retreating Boers in order to poison us. The stone helps to keep one's mouth moist when there is nothing to drink.

A F Corbett *Service through six reigns: 1891 to 1953*

Scots Guards on board a troopship to Cape Town, 1900

The following details as to diet, etc, on board a troopship, may serve to remind us of our journey out. Here is a typical day:

BREAKFAST. - About three-quarters of a pint of a curious infusion called by courtesy coffee; half-a-pound of dry bread, with now and again some half-dozen tablespoons of porridge. This is oatmeal porridge in the strictest sense, there being no other legitimate ingredient save water.

DINNER. - Three-quarters of a pint of soup (I suspect this to be water masquerading as soup on the somewhat inadequate grounds that it has been used to boil meat, puddings, or to wash greasy dishes). The meat itself is - well, we generally leave it untouched. (I never knew before where all that unwholesomely fat meat one sees at Christmas goes. I think I know now. It is used to feed the fishes on the Cape route.)

TEA. - This meal consists of a pint of 'tea' - a brew which has considerable claims to be called 'special'. It is certainly like nothing I have ever tasted before. This, with half-pound of dry bread, constitutes the last meal of the day.

No beer or spirit is procurable. There is, however, a 'dry canteen', a sort of coffee shop, which opens thrice daily for an hour. With 1,300 hungry customers, it does a roaring trade. Getting at the bar is like getting into the pit of a theatre on a first night. A 'queue' of fifty or sixty patient (!) Tommies waiting their turn is not at all an uncommon sight.

The troop deck at night is a weird picture, and it is impossible to move about save on one's hands and knees - the hammocks swing about so near the deck. The deck itself is covered with sleeping forms in more or less picturesque attitudes.

Soldiers of the Imperial Yeomanry crossing a river during the South African War, 1899-1902. NMS

Beyond the usual duties of swabbing, mess-work, guards, pickets and fatigues, there is little else to record.

After a couple of parades a day, comprising physical drill and kit inspections, the troops are at liberty to spend their time as they wish. To some, the monotony of the voyage weighs disagreeably, whilst others divide their time between reading and gazing at the wonders of the deep - spouting whales, sporting dolphins, flying fish and the gaudy miniature ship-like nautilus.

E C Moffett *With the Eighth Division*

Chocolate tin sent as a New Year gift by Scots to Scots serving in the South African war, 1900. NMS

Fish on a Friday, Black Watch, 1911

Ah widnae grumble too much about the food at Edinburgh Castle. It wis good enough but it wis rough. Ah widnae say ye got plenty of it.

Breakfast consisted generally of either a sausage - ye only got one sausage: one soldier, one sausage - or a bit o' bacon. But on the Friday ye always got a wee bit o' fish, sometimes saut fish.

This wis tae make ye buy beer. The canteen sold the beer. The canteen was in where they sell postcards at the castle now. Beer was three ha'pence a pint and ye could see the hops floatin' about on the top o' it. Oh, it wis terrible.

At the midday meal generally you got either stew or broth. Ye got broth, potatoes, and then the general fruit: prunes, rice and prunes. All good wholesome stuff.

There wis no evening meal. It wis a slice o' bread and jam. That was a ' ye got there.

There wis no supper. They yaised to put on a big can o' soup, made wi' a' the rubbish that wis left the day before, or something like that. Ye jist went in and if ye wanted it ye took it, and if ye didn't ye jist left it.

Oh, ah wis aye stervin! Ah wis a hungry man, believe me.

The canteen sold food. Ye could get a plate o' mince and tatties for 4d. I think ye could get a pie for 1d and a cup o' tea for 1d, and so on. It was quite reasonable there. So ah spent most o' ma money on food - bars o' chocolate, tae; ah wis a great chocolate eater at that time.

Ah made an allowance tae ma mother. Ah gave her 3d a day out o' ma shillin' a day pey. That left me 9d. That went mostly on food. Ah didn't smoke and ah didn't drink at that time. Ah wisnae long till I did, though!

Peter Corstorphine, in Ian MacDougall Voices from war

The Serbians sing Scots songs, World War I

Our music, or such of it as was available on gramophone records, did not seem to appeal to them [wounded Serbian soldiers] much. There was one notable exception: they loved Harry Lauder's songs, and it was not only his mirthful chuckling ones, but also the sober-sided ones. There was a quality in that lovely Scottish voice that went straight to their hearts, and soon they were lilting away blithely 'Roaming in the Gloaming' and 'I Love a Lassie'.

Isabel Elmslie, in Leah Leneman In the service of life

A Highlander meets IV Gurkhas

This day I also saw how it is possible to converse by thought transference, without interpreters, providing there is good will. ML's orderly, Janaksing, squatted under a spiny thorn bush with the batman of the CO of the Argyll and Sutherland Highlanders. They sat there for an hour and talked. At first the Jock had of course demanded to see Janaksing's *kukri*. I saw it being brandished about, and Janaksing shaking his head vigorously. He was denying that he threw it like a boomerang. Then they just talked. I wondered what medium they were using for communication, since Rifleman Janaksing Thapa spoke no English and I doubted that Private Donald Campbell had much Gurkhali. I crept closer and stretched my ears. Each soldier was speaking his own language and using few gestures - it was too hot on the rocks for violent arm-waving. I could understand both sides of the conversation, the Gurkhali better than the 'English', and it made sense. Questions were answered, points taken, opinions exchanged, heads nodded, and lips sagely pursed. When ML moved on, the two shook hands, and the Jock said, 'Abyssinia, Johnny!' He had poor Janaksing there.

John Masters Bugles and a tiger

Good advice, World War I

Hooch-Aye The following recipe for porridge has been tried and found successful in Skittish Widows' Camps: dissolve three pounds of salt in two cupfuls of water more or less according to taste: add a few lumps of oatmeal and serve as hot as conditions will permit.

Anxious Friend We know of no complete cure for serious-mindedness, but it is known that sleeping in the open air especially if exposed to bright moonlight produces a mild form of lunacy which is much to be preferred.

Indignant We entirely sympathise: it is hard lines that one should be considered to be engaged with every one with whom one passes the time of day. But in these promiscuous parts one cannot be too careful.

Chaperonage We understand that as a rule a chaperon should be at least six weeks older than oneself. A Medical Degree, however, holds good as a qualification regardless of age and wisdom.

in J G Fuller *Troop morale and popular culture*

Cleansing the multitudes, France, World War I

The bathing party of a unit was marched in, and the men went to a room where they stripped. Each man's dirty shirt and underclothing - almost always lousy - were made into one bundle, which was taken to a disinfecting chamber. The bundles were then sent off to be washed and mended by a staff of French women for reissue, when ready, to other troops. Uniforms (tunics, trousers, kilts, etc) were made into a second bundle and carried off to be turned inside out and carefully ironed along seams or pleats so as to be louse-free for the wearers after bathing was finished.

The men having bathed (which was done in the large ground floor room running the whole length of the building, by using ordinary wash-tubs set in rows and filled with hot water by a hosepipe from two big tanks heated by steam), went upstairs to another room where the clean rig-out of shirts and underclothing was now ready. Thence they passed to a third room where their uniforms, thoroughly ironed (and mended where required by a team of nimble-fingered needlewomen), were handed out to them. They then dressed and went outside to a large shed for a cup of coffee with bread and butter; and, at last, cleaned, clothed, fed and in a better mind, were marched off to rejoin their units. In a working day of ten hours a thousand men could be thus dealt with.

David Rorie *A medico's luck in the war*

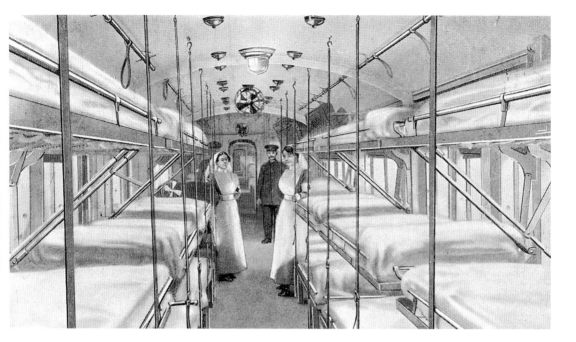

Scottish Women's Hospitals, Serbia, 1916

28 September

It was Woody's birthday today. In the morning we thought we wouldn't be able to give her anything, however, we managed. I made some tablet out of my next week's sugar ration. Ethel gave her a box of biscuits out of her home parcel, and Adam gave her a tin of milk from the store with a paper attached saying 'love from Adam and pinched with the greatest difficulty'. We also brought her a jug of hot water which she probably appreciated more than anything. This evening we had a spread of tinned orange and fruit, remnants of Colonel Wither's parcel.

Ishobel Ross *Little grey partridge*

Interior of an ambulance train built by the Caledonian Railway Company for transporting wounded soldiers in France, World War I.
NMS

Water in the desert, Egypt, 1917

We knew how to appreciate a drop of water in Sinai. Our water was brought to us in rectangular tanks (*fanatis*). A dozen or so camels with their native drivers ('Camel Transport Corps') were attached to each Battalion, and made two journeys per day to the Wady Ghuzzeh, where the engineers had sunk wells and constructed a huge reservoir. The official allowance was two

quarts per man per day, one for drinking and one for cooking, but on the subject of washing silence was observed. It went hard, however, with any man who failed to shave daily. What water there was left after bottles had been filled, was emptied into any available receptacles and used for washing purposes. A man would indulge in the luxury of a 'bath' in about three pints of water, after which he would wash any soiled articles of apparel he had and even then the 'water' would be bespoken after him by some other believer, until the remains were really beyond further use.

Bernard Blaser *Kilts across the Jordan*

Bob the dog, regimental pet of the 1st Scots Fusilier Guards, 1853-60. NMS

A heavy horse, France, World War I

Near our huts and in the ruined orchard was an interesting grave, carefully railed off, with a neatly executed wooden memorial at its head. On it the inscription ran:

TO THE MEMORY OF
BILLY THE STALLION
PET OF THE 156TH HEAVY BATTERY
KILLED BY HOSTILE AIRCRAFT
12-5-17

He was only a Blooming Heavy,
Only a Transport Horse,
But if there's a Hereafter for Horses,
Billy will not be lost.

For 2½ years we loved him,
He fought for us like a Lion,
So we've Erected this Board to Billy
For the sake of Auld Lang Syne.

The hand of the poet was, I fear, like his subject, 'blooming heavy'. But the verse was evidently the conjoint output of a committee; and a Scottish member had apparently - and with great originality - supplied the last line. Anyhow, there lay Billy, with some carefully planted chrysanthemums - where on earth had they got them? - flowering on his grave.

David Rorie *A medico's luck in the war*

Avoiding sin in Spain, 1937

One time we had a meeting at which Charlotte Haldane, Professor J B S Haldane's wife, spoke to us and greatly insulted some of our puritanical members by telling us that we had to watch out for casual women, otherwise there was a serious risk of us contracting an unpleasant disease. Some of the comrades took strong exception to this advice, coming from a woman. However advanced their political views, their moral views were puritan. I confess I was mildly amused by that.

John Dunlop, in Ian MacDougall
Voices from the Spanish Civil War

Troops in transit, 1940

A steward in white shirt and shorts holds out the breakfast menu. In the First-Class Dining Salon - for officers only - there is still peacetime service at meals. It is the only place in the liner that has suffered no change. Here, in the spaciousness, with a view of the sea through the large plate portholes, there is a daily luxury that emphasises the garbage-can life in the rest of the ship. Here there is neither war nor army, but a gathering of gentlemen sitting down to breakfast.

Glass decanter used by officers of the 94th, Scotch Brigade, about 1810. NMS

Napkins are unfolded. An officer looks at the steward and points upwards. 'Do you feel it, sir?' says the steward, adjusting the ventilator so that the stream of cooling air will avoid the immaculate hair-shed. There is a subdued clatter of cutlery and fresh white rolls are politely broken. The empty half-husk of a grapefruit is taken away and replaced with a sole meunière.

'What will you have to follow the fish, gentlemen? May I suggest the diced chicken? It is really excellent.'

... Some days ago an Orderly Officer present in the men's mess room asked in the usual way for complaints. At one table there was no verbal reply but a man handed over in silence a copy of the printed menu from the officers' mess. The man was charged with insolence.

Neil McCallum *Journey with a pistol*

Letter from Italy

From large red bugs, a refugee,
I make my bed beneath the sky,
safe from the crawling enemy
though not secure from the nimbler flea.
Late summer darkness comes, and now
I see again the homely Plough
and wonder: do you also see
the seven stars as well as I?
And it is good to find a tie
of seven stars from you to me.
Lying on deck, on friendly seas,
I used to watch, with no delight,
new unsuggestive stars that light
the tedious Antipodes.
Now in a hostile land I lie,
but share with you these ancient high
familiar named divinities.
Perimeters have bounded me,
sad rims of desert and of sea,
the famous one around Tobruk,
and now barbed wire, which way I look,
except above - the Pléiades.

Robert Garioch (1909-81)

Rationing in World War II

I started to smoke in the war. My mother used to say, 'I'm quite glad to see you smoke, because it makes you sit down for fifteen minutes.' I had to sit and smoke as if it was something terribly important. It was like a Japanese tea ceremony. A combination of things made me take up smoking. I have a very sweet tooth and there weren't enough coupons to get enough sweeties. I think a lot of us women took up smoking because we were always a wee bit hungry.

I remember going to a house one night to meet a woman with whom I was doing a number in a concert. She was there with her sister, and I'd been asked to have some tea. Of course I was looking at the pancakes, the jam and the butter, but when the woman I was to sing with passed me the butter, her sister snatched the little dish away: 'That's my butter. Give her yours. She's your guest!' I was shocked.

My husband's mother just never got used to rationing. As soon as her rations came she ate them. By the middle of the week she was putting sweeties in her tea, acid drops, anything, just to sweeten it. I never knew anybody, though, like her for making a jar of paste go so far. One of those wee jars, about four spoonfuls of paste in it, and she'd make about twelve big doorstep sandwiches with it. Since then I always have more filling than I have bread. I think it's a hangover from all that hunger.

Molly Weir, in Mavis Nicholson What did you do in the war, Mummy?

A Scotswoman in Paris, World War II

I never dared use my tobacco-card in Paris. I would have had no scruples but I lacked the courage. I think it would have been more difficult to get away with than the bread-card. Now that tobacco was rationed, except among friends most men bitterly resented women's smoking, and any tobacco-card handed over the counter by a woman would have been carefully examined. The ration was two packets of cigarettes a month and one of tobacco. As François smokes very little at the best of times, he allowed me to keep his cigarettes. But what are two packets of cigarettes a month to a hardened smoker? Soon he found himself giving up his tobacco too. To this I added the tobacco from my own fag-ends and I bought a little machine that made my cigarettes better than I could make them myself. Sometimes François brought tobacco back from Lille. Like the chicory, it was smuggled over the frontier from Belgium. There was a joke going about at this time about Gallant Little Belgium striking her breast and saying, 'As long as a blade of grass remains in Belgium, our sister France shall not lack tobacco!' But none of this got me very far and I was soon looking around for other things to smoke. I remember an evening when François asked me to make him some lime-tea. I had to confess that I had smoked it all during the week.

Janet Teissier du Cros Divided loyalties

Good plain cooking, World War II

Strange food (10 instances). This was seemingly a common difficulty. Town-bred children, used to 'fish suppers', chip potatoes and tinned foods, objected to good plain cooking. It is possible, of course, that the cooking was not always 'good'; but despite this it seems indubitable that apart from mere unfamiliarity the palates of a large number of the children were vitiated. One

A Polish soldier helps with the harvest, World War II. Sikorski Museum, London

case is recorded of children who had never eaten a boiled egg before. In this connection one sagacious observer notes that change of food, air and water made many of the children fractious until they became acclimatised.

William Boyd Bickley (ed) *Evacuation in Scotland*

English as a foreign language, World War II

It is said that a Scottish girl who was teaching a Polish soldier to speak English, pointed into the window of a greengrocer's shop and said, 'Them's aipples.'

Traditional

Cameron Highlanders, World War II

A soldier with a common name had always the last two digits of his regimental number prefixed to it. As well as the Smiths, we had of course a multitude of Camerons, Macdonalds and MacKenzies; there was an unfortunate signaller attached to D Company whose number ended 0000 and who was universally and even semi-officially known as F— all MacKenzie.

Peter Cochrane *Charlie Company*

Recreation for evacuees, World War II

The first football game took place ten days after the opening. One of the male staff from town gathered the boys and explained the game in the simplest possible way. Within fifteen minutes he was left with one boy and the ball. Yet in June 1942 the City Clinics played Nerston in a properly organised game with full football kit. The score was 4-4. Admittedly one Nerston boy stopped to pick daisies, and another scored a goal for the opposite side by kicking the ball over his head.

William Boyd Bickley (ed) *Evacuation in Scotland*

Egypt, 1942

Mary's House [a brothel] was hit one night by a bomb and there were some deaths. It is said that the military casualty lists, when they appeared, showed the deceased officers as Killed in Action.

Neil McCallum *Journey with a pistol*

Aids alert for Kenya tour troops

HIGHLANDERS URGED TO TAKE TESTS

Six hundred soldiers of the 1st Bn, the Queen's Own Highlanders, are to be urged to take Aids tests after an eight-week exercise in Kenya where the disease is rife. The battalion's medical officer requested the tests after learning that at least 40 men caught venereal disease during the visit, which included several days' leave on the coastal strip near Mombasa and Malindi which is frequented by African prostitutes.

Because soldiers cannot legally be forced to submit to blood testing, all battalion members who took part in the exercise will be 'strongly advised' to take tests next month, 12 weeks after the visit began.

... The alert has led to a special instruction that men of 2nd Bn, the Parachute Regiment, who followed out the Queen's Own Highlanders to Kenya, should not take their leave on the coast. Instead arrangements were made for them to be taken to an inland safari park.

David Graves and Neil Darbyshire,
in *The Daily Telegraph*, 8 January 1987

Campaign over army battle age continues, after the Gulf Crisis

A Borders family campaigning for the withdrawal of 17-year old soldiers from battlefield service and the splitting up of brothers deployed together are to continue their fight despite a rebuff from the Ministry of Defence.

...In his letter [the Earl of Arran, parliamentary under-secretary of state for defence] says: 'The individual soldier has received the training necessary to perform his trade effectively and this is a far more important factor than his age or the amount of time he has spent in the army.

As far as related soldiers serving together in dangerous circumstances, I am afraid that this is an inevitability with a regimental system which deliberately fosters geographical affiliations.'

Mrs Gourdie said that because of relations serving together the risk of entire families being lost in a single accident was unnecessarily great.

The Scotsman 5 March 1991

AN YE HAD SEEN WHAT I HAE SEEN

The battlefield and home fires

From *Bruce's Address to his Bannockburn Army*

For we have three great avantage.
The first is, that we have the richt,
And for the richt ilk man suld ficht.
The tother is, they are cummin here,
Forlipning in their great power,
To seek us in our awn land,
And has brocht here, richt til our hand,
Riches into so great plentee
That the poorest of you sall be
Baith richt and micht therewithal
Gif that we win, as weill may fall.
The third is that we for our livis
And for our childer and our wivis
And for the freedom of our land,
Are streinyeit in battale for to stand,
And they for their micht anerly,
And forthat they leit of us lichtly,
And for they wad destroy us all,
Makis them to ficht; bot yet may fall
That they sall rue their barganing.
And, certes, I warn you of ae thing
To happen them, as God forbeid,
Who find faintness in our deed -
Gif so that they win us openly,
They sall have on us no mercy.

John Barbour (c1320-95)

This detail from a 17th-century engraving shows Scottish archers in the bodyguard of the French king, Charles VII, on the way to his coronation in 1429. NMS

Johnnie Cope

Hey, Johnnie Cope, are ye wauking yet?
Or are your drums a-beating yet?
If ye were wauking I wad wait
To gang to the coals i' the morning.

Cope sent a challenge frae Dunbar:
'Charlie, meet me an ye daur,
And I'll learn you the art o' war
If you'll meet me i' the morning.'

When Charlie looked the letter upon
He drew his sword the scabbard from:
'Come, follow me, my merry merry men,
And we'll meet Johnnie Cope i' the morning.'

'Now, Johnnie, be as good's your word;
Come, let us try both fire and sword;
And dinna rin like a frighted bird,
That's chased frae its nest i' the morning.'

When Johnnie Cope he heard of this,
He thought it wadna be amiss
To hae a horse in readiness
To flee awa' i' the morning.

Fy now, Johnnie, get up and rin;
The Highland bagpipes mak a din;
It's best to sleep in a hale skin,
For 'twill be a bluidy morning.

When Johnnie Cope to Dunbar came,
They speered at him, 'Where's a' your men?'
'The deil confound me gin I ken,
For I left them a' i' the morning.'

'Now, Johnnie, troth, ye are na blate
To come wi' the news o' your ain defeat,
And leave your men in sic a strait
Sae early in the morning.'

'I' faith,' quo' Johnnie, 'I got a fleg
Wi' their claymores and philabegs;
If I face them again, deil break my legs!
Sae I wish you a gude morning.'

Adam Skirving (1719-1803)

The braes o' Killiecrankie

Whaur hae ye been sae braw lad
Whaur hae ye been sae brankie, O!
Whaur hae ye been sae braw lad,
Cam ye by Killiecrankie, O!

Oh an ye had been whaur I hae been,
Ye wadna been sae cantie, O!
An ye had seen what I hae seen,
On the braes o' Killiecrankie, O!

I fought at hame, I fought at sea,
At hame I fought my auntie, O!
But I met the Devil and Dundee,
On the braes o' Killiecrankie, O!

The bauld Pitcur fell in a furr,
And Clavers gat a clankie, O!
Or I hae fed an Athol gled,
On the braes o' Killiecrankie, O!

Oh fie MacKay, what gart ye lie
In the bush o' yonder brankie, O!
Ye'd better kiss King Willie's mouth
Than come by Killiecrankie, O!

There's nae shame, there's nae shame
There's nae shame tae swankie, O!
There's soor slaes on Athol braes
And the de'il's at Killiecrankie, O!

Traditional

Colours carried by Barrell's Regiment of Foot at the Battle of Culloden, 1746. NMS

A soldier's letter

My Dearest Jeannie,

I have ventured by this post, tho' it's a great chance if it come to hand. Wee arrived here last night amidst the acclamations of the people, and publick rejoicings which wee have had in severall places, and we are now within a hundred miles of London without seeing the face of one enemy, so that in a short time I hope to write you from London, where if we get safe, the whole of our story and even what has happened already must appear to posterity liker a romance than anything of truth. I still continue in good health as Mr Auckinleck and all friends do, thank God. Make our compliments to all our friends and believe me ever to be,

Dear Jeanie, your affectionate husband

Peter Auchterlony

Illustration of bayonet drill from a manual, after 1743. NMS

Front Ranks push your
Bayonets 3 times 6 Mo.

Front ranks stand fast as you are, Rear ranks march 3 paces in a line as you stand, center D: First draw up your left foot to y right heel, count 3 & 2 with y right foot, At y word of command turn your firelock as lightning over your left Arm seizing y butt & extending y right foot a little further in a line a: y left, y Rear rank fir= =ing y Cocks, as they turn over y left Arm, keeping their Elbows high to clear y front rank

The Battle of Prestonpans, 1745

The field of battle presented a spectacle of horror, being covered with hands,
legs and arms, and mutilated bodies; for the killed all fell by the sword.

The Chevalier de Johnstone *Memoirs of the rebellion in 1745, 1746*

The Battle of Falkirk, 1746

Hawley's line regiments were drawn up in two ranks with the dragoons on the left
and slightly in front. The Argyll men were posted to the right of the second rank
at the bottom of the hill and out of sight of the enemy. The Macgregors and the
Macdonalds approached within 90 feet of the dragoons before they discharged
their muskets, causing considerable slaughter and Ligonier's and Hamilton's dragoons turned tail, riding down their own infantry. Cobham's Dragoons engaged
the Jacobite centre but were repulsed and, to avoid collision with their own
troops, galloped down between the opposing lines sustaining casualties on the
way, until they reached Hawley's right wing. In the meantime the Frasers,
Camerons and Stewarts had been unable to attack the regiments on Hawley's
right because of a deep gully intervening and were only able to exchange fire with
the better Hanoverian marksmen and had fallen back a little. Cobham's dragoons
halted their flight to engage them.

It was then that Prince Charles took a hand in the action, bringing forward
the French Pickets in support. Seeing this the dragoons again took flight followed by all of Hawley's line regiments. The Argyll men, overwhelmed at the bottom of the hill could only follow suit. So precipitate was the collapse of the
Hanoverian Army that the Lord George Murray, fearing an ambush, stopped the
pursuit and only the blaze of Hawley's tents, abandoned with the baggage and
artillery in his flight, told the Jacobite general the rout was complete.

Lieut Col Campbell reported to his father the following day "... The dragoons behaved ill ... the Militia were not engaged but half of them deserted."
Among the deserters was the bard Duncan Ban Macintyre. He had been serving
in Carwhin's Glenorchy company of Militia and was actually there for payment as
substitute for Archibald Fletcher, a farmer in Crannach. As a mercenary his
motivation would normally be suspect but, in his two songs about the Battle of
Falkirk, his sympathies show very clearly. The songs are to some extent a dis-
praisal of Fletcher, who refused to pay him because Duncan had thrown away
Fletcher's sword to facilitate his flight from battle.

What Duncan does say, however, shows a remarkable insight into the course of the battle. For example,

"...Dheirich fuathas anns an ruaig dhuinn,	Panic overtook us in the rout,
Nuair a ghluais an sluagh le leathad	When the host moved downhill
Bha Prionns' Tearlach le chuid Frangach	Prince Charles and his French contingent
'S iad an geall air teachd 'n ar rathad.	were purposing to come our way.
Cha d' fhuair sinn facal command	We received no word of command
A dhiarraidh ar naimhdean a sgathadh	ordering that our foes be smitten
Ach comas sgaoileadh feadh an t-saoghail	Just leave to scatter through the land
'S cuid againn gun fhaotainn fhathast."	And some of us are missing still.

This shows that he knew that the flood of the downhill retreat which overwhelmed him was instituted by the intervention of the French Pickets, an action which he could not possibly have seen.

It is not unknown for other ranks of a defeated force to attribute the debacle to poor leadership. Elsewhere he says

"Rinn e cuideachadh d' ar naimhdean	It was an advantage to our foes
Gu robh dith chommanda oirne	That our command was defective
Cha d'fhuair sinn ordugh gu lamhach	We received no order to shoot
An uair do chach bhi tighinn 'n ar comhdail	While the enemy closed with us
'S ann a theich sinn ann ar deannaibh	Indeed we fled at speed
'S chan fhanamaid ri bhith comhla."	Waiting not to be together.

But this is exactly what Lt Col. Campbell says on the subject. He wrote to his father, the General, on the following day "...Distressed by want of officers that know their duty... some companies lost 35-40 men... Achnaba's company only one sergeant, one corporal and seven men left... Whole Militia does not exceed 350 men. Macrihanish Company all prisoners... chiefly due to the carelessness and ignorance of the officers." Campbell of Succoth wrote to the Sheriff of Argyll on 18th January, that the companies of the brothers, Melford and Achnaba "intended to cross Queensferry and go home by Doune, but I advised them to go straight to Edinburgh. I do not know how they were parted from the main body or their present whereabouts. The Colonel's Volunteer, Kilgroat, was nearly captured at Falkirk... was fund at Queensferry having stript off his regimentals... the officers were obviously escaping on horse without their troops."

As Duncan Ban says in the last piece quoted,

Cha d'fhan duine ri cheile	None of them waited for the others
Eadar Dun Eideann is Sruidhleadh	Between Edinburgh and Stirling
S iomadh baile 'san robh pairt dhuibh	There's many a town where some of them
Gabhail taimh air teachd na-oidhche	Rested when the night came

And General Campbell also echoed the opinion of the illiterate soldier bard. To the Duke of Argyle he wrote on 29th January "... The men were good. The officers, I had to take, were such as the deputy Lieutenants chose to name... did not do their duty". Writing later on, he spoke of the Militia as "the best levies I have ever seen, the officers excepted..."

Alasdair Maclean *Transactions of the Gaelic Society of Inverness*

Fraser's Regiment upon the Plains of Abraham, 1759

About 6 o'clock observed the enemy coming from town, and forming under cover of their cannon; we saw they were numerous, therefore the General made the proper disposition for battle; they marched up in one extensive line. When they came within reconoitring view they halted, advancing a few of their Irregulars, who kept bicquering with one or two platoons, who were advanced for that purpose, at the same time playing with three field pieces on our line. On which the General ordered the line to lay down till the enemy came close, when they were to rise up and give their fire. The enemy, thinking by our disappearing, that their cannon disconcerted us, they thought proper to embrace the opportunity; wheeling back from the centre, and formed three powerful columns, advanced very regular with their cannon

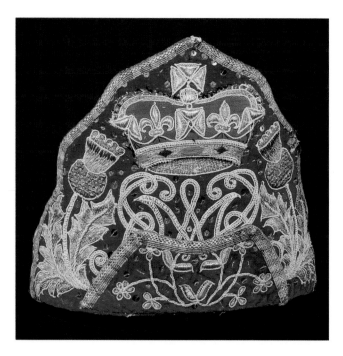

Mitre cap of a Grenadier officer in a Scottish infantry regiment, about 1690, the earliest surviving piece of Scottish military headdress. NMS

playing on us. By this time we had one field piece on the right, and two howats on the left who began to give fire; the enemy huzza'd, advancing with a short trott (which was effectually shortened to a number of them) they began their fire on the left, the whole of them reclining that way, but received and sustained such a check that the smell of gun-powder became nauseous; they broke their line, to all parts of the compass.

To our great concern and loss General Wolfe was mortally wounded; but the Brigadiers, who were also wounded, excepting Murray, seeing the enemy break, ordered the Grenadiers to charge in among them with their bayonets, as also the Highlanders with their swords, which did some execution, particularly in the pursuit.

During the lines being engaged, a body of the enemy attacked a part of the Light Infantry on the right, were repulsed and thought proper to follow the fait of traverse sailing. As I was not in the line of battle I can't say what the latest disposition of the enemy before engaging.

How soon this action was over we received a part of our intrenching tools, and began to make redoubts, not knowing but next morning we would have another to cut, as the enemy expected 13 companies of Grenadiers to join, and about 2000 men who occupy'd a post near Point au Treamp, but it seemed they were not recovered of the former morning's portion; not liking English medicines.

This affair gave great spirit to the whole army, notwithstanding the loss of the much regretted Life of the Army, General Wolfe. The men kept sober, which was a great maxim of their bravery.

An NCO of Fraser's Regiment, in A Doughty
The Siege of Quebec

A bloody bonnet, 71st Regiment, 1808

Another of our men had his bonnet driven off his head, and set on fire, by a shell; but he never stopt an instant to reflect on his miraculous escape, for, snatching up the unfortunate Sweeny's bonnet, he clapt it on his head with great *sang froid*, although it (the bonnet) contained some of the blood and brains of its former possessor.

Vicissitudes in the life of a Scottish soldier

Badajoz, 94th Scots Brigade, 1812

When the town surrendered, and the prisoners were secured, the gate leading from the town into the castle was opened, and we were allowed to enter the town for the purpose of plundering it. We were scarcely through the gate when every regiment of the division were promiscuously mixed, and a scene of confusion took place which baffles description: each ran in the direction that pleased himself, bursting up the doors and rummaging through the houses, wantonly breaking up the most valuable articles of furniture found in them. Small bands formed, and when they came to a door which offered resistance, half-a-dozen muskets were levelled at the lock, and it flew up; by this means many men were wounded, for having entered at another door, there was often a number in the house, when the door was thus blown open. The greater number first sought the spirit stores, where having drank an inordinate quantity, they were prepared for every sort of mischief. At one large vault in the centre of the town, to which a flight of steps led, they had staved in the head of the casks, and were running with their hat-caps full of it, and so much was spilt here, that some, it was said, were actually drowned in it. Farther on, a number of those who had visited the spirit store were firing away their ammunition, striving to hit some bells in front of a convent.

Les Ecossais à Paris ou la Curiosité des Femmes: *Highland soldiers captured the popular imagination during the occupation of Paris after Waterloo, 1815-18.* NMS

The effects of the liquor now began to show itself, and some of the scenes which ensued are too dreadful and disgusting to relate; where two or three thousand armed men, many of them mad drunk, others depraved and unprincipled, were freed from all restraint, running up and down the town, the atrocities which took place may be readily imagined; but in justice to the army, I must say they were not general, and in most cases perpetrated by cold-blooded villains, who were backward enough in the attack. Many risked their lives in defending helpless females, and although it was rather a dangerous place for an officer to appear, I saw many of them running as much risk to prevent inhumanity, as they did the previous night in storming the town. I very soon sickened of the noise, folly, and wickedness around me, and made out of the town towards the breach.

...The camp during that day, and for some days after, was like a masquerade, the men going about intoxicated, dressed in the various dresses they had found in the town; French and Spanish officers, priests, friars, and nuns, were promiscuously mixed, cutting as many antics as a mountebank. It was some days before the army could be brought round to its former state of discipline. Indeed the giving leave to plunder the town, was productive of nothing but bad consequences, and for the interests of humanity, and the army at large, I hope such license may never recur, should we be again plunged in war.

Joseph Donaldson *The eventful life of a soldier*

71st Highlanders, the day after Waterloo, 1815

Scarce was my body stretched upon the ground when sleep closed my eyes. Next morning when I awoke I was quite stupid. The whole night my mind had been harassed by dreams. I was fighting and charging, re-acting the scenes of the day, which were strangely jumbled with the scenes I had been in before. I rose up and looked around, and began to recollect. The events of the 18th came before me, one by one; still they were confused, the whole appearing as an unpleasant dream. My comrades began to awake and talk of it; then the events were embodied as realities. Many an action had I been in wherein the individual exertions of our regiment had been much greater and our fighting more severe; but never had I been where the firing was so dreadful and the noise so great. When I looked over the field of battle it was covered and heaped in many places, figures moving up and down upon it. The wounded crawling along the rows of the dead was a horrible spectacle; yet I looked on with less concern, I must say, at the moment, than I have felt at an accident, when in quarters. I have been sad at the burial of a comrade who died of sickness in the hospital and followed him almost in tears; yet have I seen, after a battle, fifty men put into the same trench, and comrades amongst them, almost with indifference. I looked over the field of Waterloo as a matter of course, a matter of small concern... [The 71st on 18 June had casualties of 16 officers, 11 sergeants and 187 rank and file, killed and wounded.]

In marching through the city, a lad dressed as a Frenchman was looking up the companies very anxiously. One of our men said, 'Knock the French fellow down.' 'Dinnae be sae fast, man,' said he. We stared to hear broad Scotch in Paris at this time. 'I am looking for my cousin,' he added, naming him; but he had been left behind, wounded.

When we were in the camp before the Tuilleries, the first day, two girls were looking very eagerly up and down the regiment, when we were on parade. 'Do you wish a careless husband, my dear?' said one of our lads. 'May be: will you be't?' said a Glasgow voice. 'Where the devil do you come from?' said the rough fellow. 'We're Paisley lasses; this is our regiment. We want to see if there's ony body here we ken.' The soldier, who was a Glasgow lad, could not speak. There is a music in our native tongue, in a foreign land where it is not to be looked for, that often melts the heart when we hear it unexpectedly. These two girls had found their way from Paisley to Paris, and were working at tambouring, and did very well.

Journal of a soldier of the 71st regiment

Indian Mutiny, 93rd Highlanders, 1857

Among the volunteers who came from the Seventy-Second was a man named James Wallace. He and six others from the same regiment joined my company. Wallace was not his real name, but he never took any one into his confidence, nor was he ever known to have any correspondence. He neither wrote nor received any letters and was usually so taciturn in his manner that he was known in the company as the Quaker, a name which had followed him from the Seventy-Second... During the march to Lucknow it was a common thing to hear the men in my company say they would give a day's grog to see Quaker Wallace under fire; and the time had now come for their gratification.

... When the signal for the assault was given, Quaker Wallace went into the Secundrabâgh like one of the Furies, if there are male Furies, plainly seeking death but not meeting it, and quoting the 116th Psalm, Scotch version in metre, beginning at the first verse:

> I love the Lord, because my voice
> And prayers He did hear.
> I, while I live, will call on Him,
> Who bow'd to me his Ear.

And thus he plunged into the Secundrabâgh quoting the next verse at every shot fired from his rifle and at each thrust given by his bayonet:

> I'll of salvation take the cup,
> On God's name will I call;
> I'll pay my vows now to the Lord
> Before His people all.

It was generally reported in the company that Quaker Wallace single-handed killed twenty men, and one wonders at this, remembering that he took no comrade with him and did not follow Sir Colin [Campbell]'s rule of "fighting in threes", but whenever he saw an enemy he "went for" him!

...After having carefully examined the wounds, he [Captain Dawson] noticed that in every case the men had evidently been shot from above. He thereupon stepped out from beneath the tree, and called to Quaker Wallace to look up if he could see anyone in the top of the tree, because all the dead under it had apparently been shot from above. Wallace had his rifle loaded, and stepping back he carefully scanned the top of the tree. He almost immediately called out, 'I see him, sir!' and cocking his rifle he repeated aloud: 'I'll pay my vows now to the Lord, Before His people all.' He fired and down fell a body dressed in a tight-fitting red jacket and tight-fitting rose-coloured silk trousers; and the breast of the jacket bursting open with the fall, showed that the wearer was a woman. She was armed with a pair of heavy old-pattern cavalry pistols one of which was in her belt still loaded, and her pouch was still about half-full of ammunition, while from her perch in the tree, which had been carefully prepared before the attack, she had killed more than half-a-dozen men. When Wallace saw that the person whom he had shot was a woman, he burst into tears, exclaiming: "If I had known it was a woman, I would rather have died a thousand deaths than have harmed her."

William Forbes-Mitchell Reminiscences of the Great Mutiny, 1857-1859

It's you or me, Omdurman, 1898

The incident referred to was when, after stepping over some of these bodies, I sensed some unusual movement behind me, and on looking round, caught a huge Dervish, about 6 ft. 4 ins. tall, with a thick bushy beard, getting up with a large double-handed sword. I shouted out: 'Look out, chaps', when three of my companions turned just in time to see the great fellow preparing to wield his sword with both hands, which could have sliced off at least two of our heads in one sweep. But before he could poise himself for the blow he was surrounded and our bayonets found their way into him in four different directions. I shall never forget the look in his eyes as he dropped his heavy sword and fell. I wish I could have taken a snapshot of this little 'incident'. After that, we were compelled to look into the eyes of every body on the ground, and if there was the least sign or flicker of life, he was disposed of in a similar manner, because it meant 'It's you or me, chum, and it's not going to be me.'

A F Corbett Service through six reigns: 1891 to 1953

Edinburgh, 1914

As I say, I remember vividly the outbreak of the 1914 war. There were no Sunday newspapers in those days. And my granny lived in the upper flat of the house that we were in, and I used to often spend time up there. Well, my brother and I were up there with granny this day and there was the *Dispatch* and *News* man calling across the Water of Leith from us. And I remember my granny saying, 'Either the King's deid or there's a war broken oot.' And she gave my elder brother some money to go and buy the paper - the *News*, I think. In those days it was either a halfpenny or a penny. And the news-vendor was charging sixpence for it! War profiteering!

J K Annand, in Ian MacDougall Voices from war

Gathering sphagnum moss, World War I

After he had spent three years schoolmastering at Loretto and two years as Gamma's estate manager at Craigielands, World War I broke out. My father at thirty-eight did not have any idea of joining the combatants. Instead he organised the collection and despatch of sphagnum moss for field dressings. This was his moment of glory: his organising powers were considerable and soon, with a battalion of Women's Army Corps workers at his back, he was organising sphagnum moss for the whole of Scotland. From far and wide lorries drove up to Craigielands laden with dripping sacks of moss which was spread out to dry on frames on the tennis courts. Then, after a number of simple industrial processes carried out on machines invented by my father, the moss was shredded, packed and despatched. It was said to be twenty times more absorbent than cotton wool and to have saved many lives. For his efforts with sphagnum moss my father was awarded the CBE. Nothing he ever did in his life before or after was so practical or successful.

My father was still immersed in sphagnum moss when I was born in October 1917. I do not remember the operations themselves but numerous relics of the sphagnum moss age survived as a vivid reminder of wartime life at Craigielands. All manner of sphagnum detritus was piled into the Moss

A group of people returning from gathering sphagnum moss, World War I. The moss has antiseptic properties and was used in hospitals for dressing wounds.
Scottish Life Archive

Room, a large loft where the final process had taken place. There were wooden monorails and wide flat sleepers and two wheeled wooden trolley-like giant scooters upon which the army of women had pushed sodden sacks of moss from the water-logged swamps to the lorry at the road head. There were jute sacks in their thousands, looms, frames, Heath Robinson machines of all kinds, heavy clothing for the army women as they fought their way through the Scottish winter, and in one corner, like grain in a Pharoah's tomb, a dusty pile of sphagnum moss itself.

Denis Forman *Son of Adam*

The bullet

Every bullet has its billet;
Many bullets more than one.
God! perhaps I killed a mother
When I killed a mother's son.

Joseph Lee (1878-1949)

Female munitions worker at Ness, World War I.
Scottish Life Archive

The blue of eternity, 1915

One evening when walking past the cricket nets at school, I was hit on the side of the head by a straight drive down the pitch over the bowler's head. But that was not the explanation of the singing in my ears and the crack on the head I had just received. The Germans wouldn't heave a cricket ball at me. What could it be? *Blast it*, I've been hit. I wonder what by. Couldn't have been a shell as there was no explosion. Must have been a bullet. *Damnation*, look at the blood pouring down on to my new tunic. I've been hit in the head. Has it gone through and smashed up my teeth? No, they were all there. Was the bullet in my head? If so this was the end. Meantime I had better lie down. Apart from anything else I was standing in exposed ground and if hit once could be hit again and there was no point in that. It would be nice to have a few minutes to collect myself. I stepped back a pace or two behind the parapet and lay down. I suppose this had occupied in all about four seconds, but the processes of thought and action were definite and sequential. I became aware of other people. A Wiltshire sergeant appeared; I heard him say something about a sniper in a brickstack forty yards away. He lifted up the skirt of my tunic to get my 'first field dressing'. Of course I had none on my good tunic and told him so. He was very agitated. (I wonder if he is still alive?) He tore off his own and tied it round my head but it did not seem to stop the flow of blood. I was looking straight up into the clear and cloudless blue of the sky. 'Is the major there?' I said. 'Here I am, Reith,' he replied in a trembling voice. 'Can you give me a bit of paper?' It was the Wiltshire sergeant who tore a sheet from a little notebook and handed it to me. I got out my fountain pen and in a very shaky hand wrote my mother's name and address, and then: 'I'm all right.' I did not mean what the words would obviously first suggest. But no one with such a wound as I had would be so silly as to suggest that he was 'all right' in the usual sense. I hesitated and nearly wrote the few additional words which would have made it clear; but I was sure my father and mother would see in the message what I meant them to see. 'Can you read it?' I asked the Wiltshire sergeant, for I could hardly see it myself. He read it out. Then I thought I might write in Latin the message I really wanted to send; but I let it go. I was tired and wanted to look at the sky again. The opening lines of a children's hymn came to mind:

> 'Above the clear blue sky
> In Heaven's bright abode...'

Well, very soon now the supreme mystery would be solved, I was completely content and at peace. All was well... in after years I have often wished that I could contemplate the blue of eternity with such equanimity as then.

Lord Reith *Wearing spurs*

Air an Somme

An oidhche mus deach sinn a-null
Bha i drùidhteach a' sileadh,
Bha mi fhèin 'nam laighe 'n cuil
'S thug mi sùil feadh nan gillean.

Ochan ì, ochan ì,
Tha sinn sgìth anns an ionad.
Ochan ì, ochan ì.

Cuid 'nan suidhe 's cuid 'nan suain,
Cuid a' bruadar 's a'bruidhinn,
Gu robh mhadainn gu bhith cruaidh -
'Saoil am buannaich sinn tilleadh?'

'Cha dèan biùgaileir le bheul
Ar pareudadh-ne tuilleadh;
Thèid ar dealachadh bho chèil','
Thuirt mi fhèin far mo bhilean.

Agus mar a thubhairt b'fhìor,
Chaidh na ciadan a mhilleadh,
Chaidh an talamh as a rian
'S chaidh an iarmailt gu mireag.

Dhubh an àird an ear's an iar,
Is an sliabh gu robh crith ann,
Is chan fhaighinn m'anail sìos -
Aileadh cianail an tine.

Is cha chluinninn guth san àm
Aig comanndair gar leigeil,
Bha na balaich 's iad cho trang
Cumail thall na bha tighinn.

Bha gach fear a' caogadh sùl,
'S e air cùlaibh a chruinneig,
A' cur peileir glas a-null
Le uile dhùrachd a chridhe.

On the Somme

The night before we went over
The soaking rain poured down;
I lay in a corner
And looked around the lads.

Ochan ee, ochan ee,
We are tired in this place.
Ochan ee, ochan ee.

Some sitting, some slumbering,
Some dreaming and talking,
Saying the morning would be hard -
'Do you think we can win back?'

'Never again shall a bugler
Call us on parade;
We shall be separated from one another,'
I murmured to myself.

What I said proved true.
Hundreds were maimed;
The earth erupted
And the skies went crazy.

The east and the west grew black
And the hillside shook,
And I couldn't draw in breath -
The dreadful smell of the fire.

At the time I could hear no commander
Urging us on;
The boys were fully occupied
Repelling the attacks upon us.

Each man was cocking an eye
Behind his sweetheart,*
Sending over a grey bullet
With his utmost will.

* his gun

Dòmhnall Dòmhnallach
Dòmhnall Ruadh Chorùna

51st (Highland) Division's Farewell to Sicily
Sung to the pipe tune *Farewell to the creeks*

The pipie is dozie, the pipie is fey,
He winna come round for his vino the day.
The sky ow'r Messina is unco and grey,
An' a' the bricht chaulmers are eerie.

Then fare weel, ye banks o' Sicily,
Fare ye weel, ye valley and shaw.
There's nae Jock will mourn the kyles o' ye,
Puir bluidy swaddies are wearie.
Fare weel, ye banks o' Sicily,
Fare ye weel, ye valley and shaw,
There's nae hame can smoor the wiles o' ye,
Puir bluidy swaddies are wearie.

Then doon the stair and line the waterside,
Wait your turn, the ferry's awa.
Then doon the stair and line the waterside,
A' the bricht chaulmers are eerie.

The drummie is polisht, the drummie is braw -
He cannae be seen for his webbin' ava.
He's beezed himself up for a photy an a'
Tae leave wi' his Lola, his dearie.

Sae fare weel, ye dives o' Scily
(Fare ye weel, ye shieling an' ha').
We'll a' mind shebeens and bothies
Whaur kind signorinas were cheerie.
Fare weel, ye banks o' Sicily
(Fare ye weel, ye shieling an' ha').
We'll a' mind shebeens and bothies,
Whaur Jock mde a date wi' his dearie.

Then tune the pipes and drub the tenor drum
(Leave your kit this side o' the wa').
Then tune the pipes and drub the tenor drum,
A' the bricht chaulmers are eerie.

Hamish Henderson (1919-)

Rent strike, 1917

I married during the war, in 1917. I married a man who was gassed and come back from the war. I went into a single apartment in Govan.

During the war years there was people getting put out of their homes because they couldn't pay their rent. A lot of their men were in the Forces and at that time the soldiers' allowance was a shilling a day and they got half-pay. The rent courts were full of people. And then there was what they called enrolments, re-enrolments and other re-enrolments. Sometimes the sheriff said you had to pay seven shillings. If you couldn't pay five shillings a week rent how on earth could you pay seven shillings a week?

Well, the women got together and we decided that not one soldier's wife would be put out of her home. And guided by Baillie Mary Barbour, who was a plodder and who did tremendous work - we picketed those homes. They barricaded themselves up and we picketed the homes. They couldn't put anybody out between sunset and sunrise. The picket had to be between sunrise and sunset. Then after that you could go home.

Grace Kennedy, in Ian MacDougall *Voices from war*

A baby arrives, Invergordon Mutiny, 1931

The sailors were standing abaft the breakwater and looking on, except for one remarkable moment when three of them climbed over the breakwater, marched up to me, put their hats straight, and said, 'Sir, a signal has been intercepted. Your wife and daughter are doing very well.' Having said that, they saluted again and renewed the mutiny.

Lieutenant-Commander Charles Drage, in Alan Ereira
The Invergordon mutiny

Famous faces in the Spanish Civil War

On one occasion when the anti-tank battery were situated in the hills for a week or so somewhere in the Aragon, time and place not remembered but before Franco's offensive began, I had an experience involving two inquisitive Americans. As I had been up a good part of the night I was snatching some sleep under an olive tree when I was awakened by Jimmy Arthur, a dour imperturbable Scot from Edinburgh. He was on guard and had his rifle slung over his shoulder. In his typically direct way Jimmy growled, "There's a couple o' bastards up on the trucks examining the guns." "Did you give them permission?" I asked. You just don't allow strangers under any circumstances to mess about with your guns. "No, ah didnae," said Jimmy, "the bastards jist went up on their own." When I looked at the two men on the trucks I immediately recognised Ernest Hemingway, the author, as one of them. I knew him from his photographs. The other man was an American 'lootenant' who was attached to Brigade headquarters and who flaunted his officer's uniform ostentatiously. Being a bit crabbit on being awakened out of my sleep and feeling my proletarian resentment at too much ostentatiousness, I had already formed an antipathy to the lieutenant. I growled back at Jimmy, "Well, order them off and if they don't get off, shoot them!" It was purely an expression of mood, born out of my coal pit expressions, and not an order. But the two men must have heard me for they got down off the truck at once, got into their car and drove off without a word. I remember thinking to myself at the time that a novelist's job was to write about people not things, and here were two dour Scots characters Hemingway might have got some copy from. Many years later Hemingway took his own life. I always had the feeling that Jimmy Arthur was the kind of morose character who might have saved him the bother.

Hugh Sloan, in Ian MacDougall *Voices from the Spanish Civil War*

The Tryst

She was the lassie to redd the house
And bake the scones on the fire;
He was the laddie to tent the cows
And bring them ben to the byre.
These were the twa; and sure they swore
To meet at the road-end late:
'Twas the lassie that never cam but the door,
And the laddie that gaed his gate.
A sodger laddie that stands and daffs
At the slock of a clarty close,
With a queyn o' the toun that lichtly laughs
Wi' lips as reid as a roce;
A farmer's lassie that dreams o' both,
And greets, for she canna sleep
For the bitter thought of a broken troth
And a tryst that she didna keep.

Bernard Fergusson

Looting of Italian businesses in Edinburgh when Italy enters the war, 10 June 1940

Restaurants, ice-cream shops, fish and chip shops, hairdresser's establishments and the premises of a firm of wine-importers had their windows smashed... The police did their best to bring the more hot-headed elements to reason, but they had a more or less impossible job. The wrecking activities seemed to be led by a comparatively small number of irresponsible young men, and the majority of the crowd seemed to be content to stand by and shout and follow on to the next scene of operations. Many expressions of sympathy for the occupants of the shops were heard, as it was known that some of the shopkeepers were British subjects, and indeed the proprietor of one well known restaurant whose premises were among the most seriously damaged in the city, fought throughout the last war in the ranks of a Scottish regiment.... By this forenoon 160 Edinburgh men between the ages of 16 and 70 had been sent to internment camps.

Edinburgh Evening Dispatch 11 June 1940

Portrait of Lance-Corporal Robertson, 11th City of Edinburgh Battalion Home Guard, by Eric Kennington, 1943.

Back home to Edinburgh, 1946

Goin' home was emotional, it was strange. I'd known by this time my mother was actually operatin' an overhead crane in Redpath Brown's Engineering Company down at Easter Road. My mother! I couldnae believe it. So I had to go and see this, of course. So ah walks in uniform into Redpath Brown through the workshop and: 'There she's up there, son.' And there was my mother up in the roof. I would never have believed it, I would never have believed it. She was copin'. She was quite happy. Och, she must have been then well intae her forties. She'd been married quite young. Well, she waved down to me then she climbed down and had a wee crack wi' me. She was wearin' a boiler suit, and a turban round her hair, operatin' this crane. Handlin' tons and tons o' metal, swinging it over these guys' heads. I said, 'I wouldnae work under there!'

Eddie Mathieson, in Ian MacDougall *Voices from war*

Smiling members of the Women's Forestry Service, possibly at Sorbie in Wigtownshire, World War II. Scottish Life Archive

Difficulties of Householders and Evacuees, World War II

The inability of evacuees to adjust themselves to their new environment (27 instances). This is the reason most commonly given on the side of the evacuees. Town dwellers did not take to the country. They missed their neighbours, their ordinary occupations and their amusements, and they found the country boring. 'There's too much grass about,' said one woman. Sometimes they were upset by expressions of contempt on the part of country people who thought little of townspeople and did not hesitate to say so. Time sometimes rectified matters, but the majority did not give time any chance to work.

William Boyd Bickley (ed) *Evacuation in Scotland*

Courage in the Royal Air Force, World War II

If ye didn't go out on a raid yerself your documents were marked LMF - Lack of Moral Fibre. You were taken right off the squadron. And you were sent any place, out the road. I objected to that sytem actually. I objected aboot it to the Commanding Officer quite strongly. Mind you, we could do that. There wis a certain freedom o' speech. We could do that. But ah said nobody

Four brothers in uniform, Royal Air Force, World War II. They are, from left to right, Flying Officer Lord David Douglas-Hamilton, Wing Commander The Duke of Hamilton, Wing Commander Lord George Nigel Douglas-Hamilton and Squadron Leader Lord Malcolm Douglas-Hamilton. They were the only four brothers in the RAF to be professional flying instructors and Squadron Leaders: three of them became Group Captains.
Lord James Douglas-Hamilton

Watercolour of a Lancaster bomber by R Hannah, World War II. NMS

knows your breakin' point. What's the breakin' point for one person is not necessarily the breakin' point for another one. And if a man's done six or seven raids, or even if he's only done two, and then he finds he cannae do any more then there's no lack o' moral fibre. That man has went his limit. And that LMF should never have happened. But it did.

In ma squadron ah remember one lad, Pete. It wis just after D-Day. And he had been goin' back and forward and the next time he come in he says, 'Ah'm tired. Ah don't want tae go. Ah'm tired.' And they said, 'Aw, you're yellow.' He said, 'Ah'm tired.' But they took an Australian lad. Now Pete was the rear gunner but the mid-upper gunner went intae the rear turret and the Australian lad went intae the mid-upper. Well, they took a direct hit and his head was blown off him. So, if Pete had been in the plane, obviously, all other things bein' equal, well, it wouldnae have been him, but the other gunner would have been in the mid-upper turret. But Pete was accused of Lack of Moral Fibre. And ah remember goin' intae the mess that day and Pete was sittin' at the table. We a' had our own tables actually. But ah knew ma crew wouldnae be comin' in so ah just sat down beside him. And Pete said, 'You'll be gettin' intae trouble for sittin' here, Bill.' Ah said, 'What for?' He said, 'Ah've been sent tae Coventry.' Ah said, 'What for?' So he telt me. And right enough up come a lad and said tae me, 'Excuse me, you're no' supposed tae be speakin tae him.' Ah says, 'And whae are you?' He says, 'Oh, ah've been sent across tae tell you.' Ah says, 'Who are you and who sent you across?' 'Ah well,' he says, 'Pete didnae go up and somebody else was killed in heez place.' Ah says, 'So what are you wantin' Pete tae do? Commit suicide?' Ah says, 'Away and go and rap off.' Ah says, 'When you've done as many operations as Pete's done you come and tell me. 'And', ah says, 'when you've done as many operations as ah've done ye'll be dead.' I'd done twenty-seven by then.

There was no lack of sympathy among the crews for somebody who just felt tired and couldn't carry on. It's the old thing that ye see if they show ye an old war film aboot a man gettin' shot for cowardice. It wis only tae boost up some officer's ego. It wis only the common ordinary man that wid be a coward, not an officer. So they shot the private that wis runnin' in the wrong direction. Now the same thing applied in the bombers. When somebody gets tae the stage that they cannae go intae an aeroplane it's not because they're a coward but because they've given their all. They cannae do any more. And, oh, that happened a lot more than what has been made public.

Bill King, in Ian MacDougall *Voices from war*

THE FLOWERS OF THE FOREST

Death and mourning

Wallace's lament for Graham

Engraving of General Alexander Leslie, who served in the Swedish Army for 30 years, and was General of the Scottish Army in Ireland in 1642. NMS

When they him fand, and gude Wallace him saw,
He lichtit doun, and hint him frae them aw
In armis up; behaldand his paill face,
He kissit him, and cryit full oft, 'Allace!
My best brother in warld that evir I had!
My aefald freind when I was hardest stad!
My hope, my heill, thou was in maist honour!
My faith, my help, strenthiast in stour!
In thee was wit, freedom, and hardiness;
In thee was truth, manheid, and nobilness;
In thee was rewll, in thee was governans;
In thee was vertu withoutin varians;
In thee lawtie, in thee was great largeness;
In thee gentrice, in thee was stedfastness.
Thou was great cause of winning of Scotland,
Thoch I began, and tuke the weir on hand.
I vow to God, that has the warld in wauld,
Thy dead sall be to Southeron full dear sauld.
Martyr thou art for Scotlandis richt and me;
I sall thee venge, or ellis tharefore to dee.

Blind Harry (1450-93) from *The Actes and Deidis of the Illustre and Vallyeant Campioun Schir William Wallace*

The Highland widow's lament

O I am come tae the low countrie,
Ochone, ochone, ochrie,
Wi'out a penny in my purse
Tae buy a meal tae me.

It was na sae in the Hielan hills,
Ochone, ochone, ochrie,
Nae woman in the country wide
Sae happy was as me.

I was the happiest o a the clan,
Sair, sair may I repine,
For Donald was the bravest man,
And Donald he was mine.

Till Charlie he cam ower at last,
Sae far, tae set us free,
My Donal's arm it wanted was,
For Scotland for me.

Their waefu fate what need I tell?
Right tae the wrong did yield,
My Donald and his country fell
Upon Culloden field.

I hae nocht left me ava,
Ochone, ochone, ochrie,
My winsome Donald's dirk and brand
Intae their hands tae gie.

Ochone, ochone, O Donald O,
Ochone, ochone, ochrie,
Nae woman in this whole warld wide
Sae wretched now as me.

Traditional

The Battle of Culloden,
*by Ernest Griset after
David Morier, 1746.* NMS

The Flowers of the Forest

I've heard the lilting at our yowe-milking,
Lasses a-lilting before the dawn of day;
But now they are moaning in ilka green loaning -
The Flowers of the Forest are a' wede away.

At buchts, in the morning, nae blythe lads are scorning,
The lasses are lonely, and dowie, and wae;
Nae daffin', nae gabbin', but sighing and sabbing,
Ilk ane lifts her leglen and hies her away.

In hairst, at the shearing, nae youths now are jeering,
The bandsters are lyart, and runkled, and gray;
At fair, or at preaching, nae wooing, nae fleeching -
The Flowers of the Forest are a' wede away.

A ploughman pauses for remembrance at Smedheugh, Selkirkshire, Armistice Day, 1933. Scottish Life Archive

At e'en, at the gloaming, nae swankies are roaming,
'Bout stacks wi' the lasses at bogle to play;
But ilk ane sits drearie, lamenting her dearie -
The Flowers of the Forest are a' wede away.

Dule and wae for the order sent our lads to the Border!
The English, for ance, by guile wan the day;
The Flowers of the Forest, that focht aye the foremost,
The prime o' our land, are cauld in the clay.

We'll hear nae mair lilting at our yowe-milking,
Women and bairns are heartless and wae;
Sighing and moaning on ilka green loaning -
The Flowers of the Forest are a' wede away.

Jean Elliott (1727-1805)

The funeral of Olive Smith,
Scottish Women's Hospital, Serbia, 1916

7 October

An enemy plane over the camp today. Bits of shrapnel from the anti-aircraft guns were falling all round us in the camp.

Dr Bennett came back from Salonika and after the service tonight she told us about the funeral. There was a Serbian guard of honour, and several emblems of flowers. Among them was one from the 3rd Serbian Army tied up in red, white and blue ribbon on which was written 'In memory of a generous English friend who gave her life for us'. She was buried between two British soldiers.

Dr Bennett read us the oration that Captain Stephanovitch gave over Smithy's coffin first in English and then in Serbian. They are words I would always want to remember so I am writing down part of it.

'Friends, it is a sad duty which I have to perform, to say the last adieu to a generous friend of our people, to say it in the names of all those whom she came to help and for whom she suffered death. Through unselfish devotion and pity for our pains and sufferings, she came to us from her great country, she came to soften the hard fate of a small and most unhappy people, and she shared it to the last.'

Ishobel Ross Little grey partridge

The Soldier's Dream, music cover for a song by Thomas Campbell, Crimean period. Scottish Life Archive

A sonnet

When you see millions of the mouthless dead
Across your dreams in pale battalions go,
Say not soft things as other men have said,
That you'll remember. For you need not so.
Give them not praise. For, deaf, how should they know
It is not curses heaped on each gashed head?
Nor tears. Their blind eyes see not your tears flow.
Nor honour. It is easy to be dead.
Say only this. 'They are dead.' Then add thereto,
'Yet many a better one has died before.'
Then, scanning all the o'ercrowded mass, should you
Perceive one face that you loved heretofore,
It is a spook. None wears the face you knew.
Great death has made all his for evermore.

Charles Hamilton Sorley (1895-1915)

Home thoughts from abroad (1917)

After the war, says the papers, they'll no be content at hame,
The lads that hae feucht wi' death twae 'ear i' the mud and the rain and
    the snaw;
For aifter a sodger's life the shop will be unco tame;
They'll ettle at fortune and freedom in the new lands far awa'.

No me!
By God! No me!
Aince we hae lickit oor faes
And aince I get oot o' this hell,
For the rest o' my leevin' days
I'll mak a pet o' mysel'.
I'll haste me back wi' an eident fit
And settle again in the same auld bit.
And oh! the comfort to snowk again
The reek o' my mither's but-and-ben,
The wee box-bed and the ingle neuk
And the kail-pat hung frae the chimley-heuk!
I'll gang back to the shop like a laddie to play,
Tak doun the shutters at skreigh o' day,
And weigh oot floor wi' a carefu' pride,

And hear the clash o' the countraside.
I'll wear for ordinar' a roond hard hat,
A collar and dicky and black cravat.
If the weather's wat I'll no stir ootbye
Wi'oot an umbrella to keep me dry.

I think I'd better no tak a wife -
I've had a' the adventure I want in life. -
But at nicht, when the doors are steeked, I'll sit,
While the bleeze loups high frae the aiken ruit,
And smoke my pipe aside the crook,
And read in some douce auld-farrant book;
Or crack wi' Davie and mix a rummer,
While the auld wife's pow nid-nods in slum'er;
And hark to the winds gaun tearin' bye
And thank the Lord I'm sae warm and dry.

When simmer brings the lang bricht e'en,
I'll daunder doun to the bowling-green,
Or delve my yaird and my roses tend
For the big floo'er-show in the next back-end.
Whiles, when the sun blinks aifter rain,
I'll tak my rod and gang up the glen;
Me and Davie, we ken the püles
Whaur the troot grow great in the howes o' the hills;
And, wanderin' back when the gloamin' fa's
And the midges dance in the hazel shaws,
We'll stop at the yett ayont the hicht
And drink great wauchts o' the scented nicht,
While the hoose lamps kin'le raw by raw
And a yellow star hings awer the law.
Davie will lauch like a wean at a fair
And nip my airm to make certain shüre
That we're back frae yon place o' dule and dreid,
To oor ain kind warld -
But Davie's deid!
Nae mair gude nor ill can betide him.
We happit him doun by Beaumont toun,
And half o' my hert's in the mools aside him.

John Buchan (1875-1940)

In Flanders Fields

In Flanders fields the poppies blow
Between the crosses, row on row
That mark our place; and in the sky
The larks, still bravely singing, fly
Scarce heard amid the guns below.

We are the Dead. Short days ago
We lived, felt dawn, saw sunset glow,
Loved and were loved, and now we lie
In Flanders fields.

Take up our quarrel with the foe:
To you from failing hands we throw
The torch; be yours to hold it high.
If ye break faith with us who die
We shall not sleep, though poppies grow
In Flanders fields.

John McCrae

Pictish stone depicting soldiers in Aberlemno churchyard, about AD 500. NMS

Kinraddie, 1918-19

And that made the minister no more well-liked with Kinraddie's new gentry, you may well be sure. But worse than that came; he'd been handed the money, the minister, to raise a memorial for Kinraddie's bit men that the War had killed. Folk thought he'd have a fine stone angel, with a night-gown on, raised up at Kinraddie cross-roads. But he sent for a mason instead and had the old stone circle by Blawearie loch raised up and cleaned and set all in place, real heathen-like, and a paling put round it. And after reading his banns on that Sunday the minister read out that next Saturday the Kinraddie Memorial would be unveiled on Blawearie brae, and that he expected a fine attendance, whatever the weather - *they'd to attend in ill weather, the folk that fell.*

...The minister held open the gate for Chris and through she came, all clad in her black, young Ewan's hand held fast in hers, he'd grown fair like his father, the bairn, dark-like and solemn he was. Chris's face was white and solemn as well except when she looked at the minister as he held the gate open, it was hardly decent the look that she gave him, they might keep their courting till the two were alone. Folk cried *Ay, minister!* and he cried back cheerily and went striding to the midst of the old stone circle, John Brigson was standing there with his hands on the strings that held the bit clout.

[105]

The minister said, *Let us pray*, and folk took off their hats, it smote cold on your pow. The sun was fleering up in the clouds, it was quiet on the hill, you saw young Chris stand looking down on Kinraddie with her bairn's hand in hers. And then the Lord's Prayer was finished, the minister was speaking just ordinary, he said they had come to honour the folk whom the War had taken, and that the clearing of this ancient site was maybe the memory that best they'd have liked. And he gave a nod to old Brigson and the strings were pulled and off came the clout and there on the Standing Stone the words shone out in their dark grey lettering, plain and short:

> FOR : THE : MEMORY : OF : CHA
> RLES : STRACHAN : JAMES :
> LESLIE : ROBERT : DUNCAN :
> EWAN : TAVENDALE : WHO :
> WERE : OF : THIS : LAND : AND :
> FELL : IN : THE : GREAT : WAR :
> IN : FRANCE : REVELATION :
> II CH : 28 VERSE

Lewis Grassic Gibbon *Sunset song*

David Niven leaves Malta

'Sixty' Smith, who had become my friend and adviser, was ill in hospital. It had started with sandfly fever, then complications and now he was much more sick than anybody realised. Pleurisy had set in and there was no question of him sailing home with the rest of us. I went to see him the day before we embarked on the troopship and was shocked by his appearance.

'Would you ask the Colonel a favour for me, sorr? Would ye ask if the battalion could march a wee bit oot the road on their way tae the Dock so I can hear the pipes for the last time - it's nae far... aboot five minutes.'

I suddenly felt chilly in the warm little room. 'What the hell are you talking about, Sixty?... hearing the pipes for the last time?' 'Becos I'm gonna dee,' Sixty replied quietly and I found it impossible to look into his clouded eyes.

The Weasel was oddly sympathetic to the request and when he gave me the answer he told me the Colonel had added that he would like me to be with the old man when the troops passed the hospital the following day.

It was late afternoon when they passed and the sun was golden on the church spires that Sixty could see from his bed. In the distance he could hear the swinging march: 'Wi' a Hundred Pipers...' and he asked me to prop him up in his bed. Nearer and nearer came the battalion and as he lifted his head to listen, he must have been thinking of a whole lifetime in the regiment he had joined as a boy. Just before the column reached the hospital, the tune changed: changed to the regimental march - 'Scotland the Brave' - and tears of pride slid down his granite cheeks. He sat bolt upright till the last stirring notes faded away into the distance, then he slid down into his bed and turned his face to the wall.

That night Sixty died.

David Niven *The moon's a balloon*

from *Clemency ealasaid July 1940*

Naomi Mitchison had a stillborn daughter during World War II

...In a hundred years
The French sailors at Oran, the Scottish dead at Abbeville,
The tortured in the concentration camps and all the leaders,
The ones who thought themselves godlike, forgetting the Boyg,
And I, and my children, and all the people of Carradale,
We shall be dead, at last out of the running of events and hours.
The page will have been turned,
The history written, and we, anonymous,
Shall be condemned or not condemned, gently upbraided
For folly of not foreseeing, for dithered watching of hours
While the roughest day runs by.
But the trees I planted in the heavy months, carrying you,
Thinking you would see them grown, they will be tall and lovely:
Red oak and beech and tsuga, grey alder and douglas:
But not for you or your children. What will it matter then, forgotten
    daughter,
Forgotten as I shall be forgotten in the running of time,
Maybe a name in an index, but not me, remembered
As I alone remember, with what tears yet, the first kiss, the faint warmth
    and stirring?
The waves will cover us all diving into darkness out of the bodies of
    death,
Vanishing as the wake of a boat in a strong current.
The hot tears will be cooled and the despair of the middle-aged,
rolling up their map,
Will be forgotten, with other evil things, will be interpreted,
Will be forgiven at last.

Naomi Mitchison (1897-), from *The bull calves*

Nocht o' mortal sicht - 1942

A' day aboot the hoose I work,
My hands are rouch, my banes are sair,
Though it's a ghaist comes doon at daw,
A ghaist at nicht that clims the stair.

For nocht o' mortal sicht I see -
But warrin' tanks on ilka hand,
And twistit men that lie sae still
And sma', upon the desert sand.

And nocht I hear the leelang day
But skirl o' shell and growl o' gun,
And owre my heid the bombers roar
Reid-hot aneath the Libyan sun.

But when the licht is on the wane,
And antrin winds gae whinnerin' by,
It's snaw comes swirlin' round my feet
And drifts in clouds across the sky.

And syne it's straikit owre wi' bluid,
And syne the wind is hairse wi' cries,
And syne abune the Russian snaws
I see the Kremlin towers rise.

While round the city, mile on mile,
The grim battalions tak' their stand,
And deid men streik from aff the grund
To grup their comrades by the hand.

And sae it haps that ilka day
Frae mornin' licht to gloamin' fa'.
It is a ghaist that walks the hoose
And casts its shadow on the wa'.

Bessie J B MacArthur

The Mither's Lament

What care I for the leagues o sand,
The prisoners and the gear they've won?
My darlin liggs amang the dunes
Wi mony a mither's son.

Doutless he deed for Scotland's life;
Doutless the statesman dinna lee;
But och tis sair begrutten pride
And wersh the wine o victorie!

Sydney Goodsir Smith (1915-75)

Mementos, Burma, World War II

Not a word was said about Tich Little, but a most remarkable thing happened (and I saw it repeated later in the campaign) which I have never heard of elsewhere, in fact or fiction, although it must be as old as war.

Tich's military effects and equipment - not, of course, his private possessions, or any of his clothing - were placed on a groundsheet, and it was understood that anyone in the section could take what he wished. Grandarse took one of his mess-tins; Forster, his housewife, making sure it contained

Medals and in memoriam *card of Private Alexander Keay, Royal Army Medical Corps, killed in action at Ypres Salient, 5 October 1917.* NMS

only Army issue and nothing personal; Nixon, after long deliberation, took his rifle, an old Lee Enfield shod in very pale wood (which surprised me, for it seemed it might make its bearer uncomfortably conspicuous); I took his pialla, which was of superior enamel, unlike the usual chipped mugs. Each article was substituted on the groundsheet with our own possessions - my old pialla, Forster's housewife, and so on - and it was bundled up for delivery to the quartermaster. I think everyone from the original section took something.

It was done without formality, and at first I was rather shocked, supposing that it was a coldly practical, almost ghoulish proceeding - people exchanging an inferior article for a better one, nothing more, and indeed that was the pretext. Nick worked the bolt, squinted along the sights, hefted the rifle, and even looked in its butt-trap before nodding approval; Grandarse tossed his old mess-tin on to the groundsheet with a mutter about the booger's 'andle being loose. But of course it had another purpose: without a word said, everyone was taking a memento of Tich.

George MacDonald Fraser *Quartered safe out here*

Mute with complaint

Written after finding the body of a nineteen-year-old Marine on the sand dunes at
Walcheren, November 1944

Mute with complaint I lie
On the cold sand
And not a word is spoken
For a full hour now;
No movement save the wind
Ruffling the manes of the sand
Up there -
It was quite sudden:
The battle stilled to dimness;
No tracer more ripped through the ragged remnants of
    the brain,
And even the parabolas of sound
That herald mortars
Grew dim and puny on the far dunes.
Here I lie,
While the wind blows round the corner of my house
Silts up the sills with the drift,

Drifting sand,
Fumbles feebly with the ashes
On the cold hearth.

Tomorrow no-one will come
Curiously peeping
Through shutterless windows,
Nor try the door.
And I will be afraid
That there is none to see
No one to come,
None to be cheerful in the silent rooms.
I will be eager to leave,
Quit my tenancy
Because my house is become no house.

On the day after,
They will put it away,
Lifting with passionless hands,
Shaking off minute rivers
Of sand.
For tenantless houses are horror to living men.
I shall stand
Just near - beyond the gate
While they conceal the roof
And the walls
And the hearth and the rooms
And I will watch them go away
Back to the drift of the sand.
But I will know,
No more than now
What has really happened to me
Nor whom I am
Nor whither going.

Donald A Gibson

ARMISTICE

Peace and the aftermath of war

Discharged from the Royal Artillery, 1814

At length, I rejoice to say, the year 1814 arrived. It was evident the war was soon to be at an end, as my hopes from my father had for some months been. A reduction was ordered; and harassed and dispirited 'Old Ceylon'* was marked for his discharge.

In the month of October I was again forced to go into the hospital with an excessive pain in my head, for which many remedies were tried before it yielded to medicine. During my convalescence, the medical board sat, before which I attended; Dr. Jamieson, the surgeon-general, examined me, putting several questions as to my length of time in the regiment, and service, which I answered. 'Well, my man,' he said, 'you will get your discharge and one shilling per day.' My heart began to swell. I had arrived at last, in spite of all my exertions, to the much dreaded point 'a poor old pensioner'. The shilling per day, I thought, at this time, a secondary consideration; yet I could not help thinking it too little, as none of the Artillery I had the command of from Ceylon got less in 1811, some of whom had not been so long in the army at that time as I had been, and never were non-commissioned officers; some had been more than once flogged; and now, after four more years more service, to get just the same pension as these privates I could not think equal justice; but the money, I cared not much about, as I meant to be off for the West Indies as soon as I was free.

If such were my thoughts when I passed, how chagrined did I feel when my discharge arrived from the Ordnance Office on the 31st December 1814, and a pension of only ninepence per day.

No sooner had I got my discharge in my pocket than I felt I was a new man; I was once more free; I actually thought I stood a few inches higher, as I stretched myself like one who has just laid down a heavy load. I tarried not long in Dublin, but with the first opportunity set off for Scotland again.

* 'Old Ceylon' was aged thirty-four

Alexander Alexander *The life of Alexander Alexander*

The Black Watch celebrate on their return to Edinburgh after Waterloo

We entered the castle, proud of the most distinguished reception that ever a regiment had met with from a grateful country. Two nights we were admitted free to the Theatre, two to the Olympic Circus, two days to the panoramic view of Waterloo; and, to conclude our triumphal rejoicings, after removing from the castle to Queensberry House Barracks, an entertainment was provided for us in the Assembly Rooms, George's Street, to which the noblemen and gentlemen contributors came, and witnessed the glee with which we enjoyed their hospitality. The drink was of the best, and fame tells a lie, if the beer was not mixed with strong-ale or spirits; and so plentifully was it supplied by active waiters, during the dinner, that before the cloth was withdrawn, we were very hearty. We enjoyed the glass till nearly sunset, by which

Soldiers and staff at Whitehill Military Hospital near Dalkeith, 1915. NMS

The Battle of VITTORIA.

Pub.ᵈ by J. Sidebotham

*Satirical print of the
Battle of Vittoria, 1815,
which ended Napoleon's
domination over Spain.*
NMS

time there was scarcely a man at the table but thought himself qualified to sing a song, make a speech, or give a toast, and not a few attempted to do the whole; and, if we had been allowed an hour's longer enjoyment, the heroes of Waterloo would have been prostrated under that table, at which they had so lately sat in glorious glee, and all their laurels scattered in the dust!

We staggered out, bonnets falling off in all directions, got into our ranks, and marched off as if a whirlwind had been blowing amongst us and sweeping us out of our ranks.

We reached the North Bridge without leaving a man behind, but there we began to drop in couples, and although it was a calm pleasant afternoon, our heads were knocking against the balustrades of the bridge, as if driven upon them by the violence of a tempest. By the time our front files got to our barracks, the rear was broken, and groping and sprawling their way down the High Street. No lives were lost, though many a bonnet and kilt changed owners, and not a few disappeared entirely.

James Anton *Retrospect of a military life*

Social change in Scotland after Waterloo, 1815

We were inundated this whole winter with a deluge of a dull ugly colour called Waterloo *bleu*, copied from the dye used in Flanders for the calico of which the peasantry make their small frocks or blouses. Every thing new was Waterloo, not unreasonably, it had been such a victory, such an event, after so many years of exhausting suffering. And as a surname to hats, coats, trowsers, instruments, furniture, it was very well - a very fair way of trying to perpetuate the return of tranquillity; but to deluge us with that vile indigo, so unbecoming even to the fairest! It was really a punishment. Our *Albert* blue of this day is worth the wearing but that Waterloo was an infliction, none of us were sufficiently patriotick to deform ourselves by trying it. The fashions were remarkable ugly this season. I got nothing new, as I went out so little, till the spring, when white muslin frocks were the most suitable dress for the small parties then given. There was a dearth of news, too, a lull after the war excitement; or my feeling stupid might make all seem stupid. I know my memory recollects this as a disagreeable winter ... The country was filled with half pay Officers, many of them returned wounded to very humble homes in search of a renewal of the health they had bartered for glory. A few of these had been raised to a rank they were certainly far from adorning; very unfit claimants got commissions occasionally in those war days. Lord Huntly had most improperly advanced one or two of his servants and several of his servants' sons, and in the German legion there had been two lieutenants who began life as carpenters' apprentices to Donald Mclean. One of these, Sandy McBean, who lived the rest of his days at Guislich under the title of the *Offisher*, attended the church very smart, and dined once every season at our table, as was now his due, had helped to alter the staircase with the same hands that afterwards held his sword. Wagstaffe's son rose to be a Major. When he got his Company the father resigned his Stewardship, and received some situation from the Marquis more suited to the son's position.

Elizabeth Grant of Rothiemurchus
Memoirs of a Highland lady

Hungry and unfit after the Boer War, 1900

We soon reached the convalescent hospital at Cape Town, and after recovering some of my strength I became so hungry I felt as if could have eaten a boiled boot. I sold my watch and chain to a Royal Army Medical Corps orderly (R.A.M.C.) who are really Military Hospital nurses, for 30s; it was well worth £5, and before I left the hospital he was in possession of my watch and chain and the 30s. for extra bits of food. A shilling for a bit of butter, 6d. for extra bread, etc.etc. No wonder we called him the 'Rob All My Comrades'

Anyhow, by the time I was placed on board a homeward bound transport ship I was penniless, and peeled potatoes for nearly all the 6,000 miles home in the galley (ship's cook-house) to get extra food. After being starved while the fever is on, one gets so ravenous when well enough, one could eat almost anything.

When we arrived at Portsmouth we were sent to a 'clearing' hospital at Gosport. I was several times mistaken for a Boer prisoner because of my greasy khaki suit and beard. Several of us had them photographed before having them cut off.

After being sent to Fort George, N.B., to be medically examined for further duties, I was eventually discharged with defective eyesight, being the after-effects of the fever, etc.

I was granted a pension of 9d per day from 'a grateful country for services rendered'. I am now (1953) quite blind in one eye; the other is not so bad, but is gradually going, although I drive my car every day, but not at night.

A F Corbett *Service through six reigns: 1891 to 1953*

Men of the Imperial Yeomanry in camp, South African War, 1899-1902. NMS

Long-awaited news, Egypt, 1918

On peering into the tent to watch these men, all intent upon their game, it would have been difficult to imagine that anything unusual was in the air. But that something extraordinary was about to happen, or had actually happened, was certain from the sudden arrival of a man very much out of breath with the haste he had made, and evidently bursting with news to tell. He rushed into the tent, caught his foot in some equipment, and sprawled headlong over the cards and players, raising a torrent of remonstration.

"Armistice signed," he spluttered, after he had spat out a mouthful of sand.

But these hardened campaigners had heard this before. They had even been told to expect the "cease hostilities" signal in the form of blue Very Lights when wallowing in the mud of France in 1916.

"Don't you hear? Armistice has been signed," the new-comer repeated with emphasis.

"I didn't know they had any beer in the canteen," caustically remarked one of the players as he collected the scattered cards.

"You're ten years too soon," said one of the chess enthusiasts, looking up from the board.

The bearer of the best news they had heard for years glanced from one to another with an injured look upon his face, and becoming exasperated at the incredulity displayed, went to great pains in relating how, as he was passing the camp notice-board five minutes before, he had seen a large crowd clamouring round it striking matches in order to read a news telegram. He had not been able to get near enough to read the news himself, but had learned that an Armistice had been signed and hostilities had ceased.

At that moment another man arrived, also suffering considerably from loss of breath, who corroborated the intelligence that official news had really come through of an Armistice in all theatres of war.

"Well, I'm blowed," said one of the amazed listeners.

"At last," softly murmured another, with a sigh which spoke volumes.

"And quite time too," rejoined a third, giving it as his firm opinion that it was high time mankind stopped fighting and destroying, and settled down to decent civilized life again, employing itself upon some useful occupation for the betterment of the world generally.

"Hand round the doings, Jim," said the idealist, and the cards were dealt again, pipes and cigarettes were lit, and the chess board set to rights after the disturbance; no hilarity, no wild manifestation, no idiotic excesses.

A few rockets were sent up from the neighbouring aerodrome and the men across at the railway set fog signals on a length of line and ran a locomotive over them; but that was all. The troops to whom this glad news meant so much, received it quietly and soberly. All were deeply immersed in their own thoughts, and if we but knew, their hearts were lifted up that night in thankfulness to God for bringing to an end the horrible bloodshed, suffering and destruction that had ravaged the world for four weary years.

Bernard Blaser *Kilts across the Jordan*

Good news after the Spanish Civil War

While I was in Spain I was reported dead, I was reported killed. I didn't know anything about this until I got home. But my mother got a notice - I suppose it would be from Fred Douglas's wife, that was the job she had, to tell the parents or the wives of the men who had died. The report was that I had been killed on the Aragon front. So she got that on my birthday. I have the death certificate still, signed by Copic, who was the chief of the army group at that time. My mother collected £10 off the death insurance from Pearl Assurance Company. But some notice must have got through to the papers that I was not dead, it was a false alarm. Of course she didn't pay the money back.

George Drever, in Ian MacDougall *Voices from the Spanish Civil War*

The wild ways

How many times, in the late 'forties and 'fifties, did one see a sober citizen in his office throw aside his pencil and stare at the window and exclaim: "Oh, God, I wish the war was still on!" It is a strange echo now: who could possibly want to be at war? Nobody in his right mind, and of course the sober citizen wasn't longing for battle and sudden death, but remembering the freedom of service life, the strange sights and smells of places just like this, the uncertainty of tomorrow, and the romance of distant lands and seas. They have their hazards, but once you've trodden the wild ways you never quite get them out of your system.

George MacDonald Fraser *Quartered safe out here*

Prejudice against conshies, after World War II

The only thing I might add, as an aftermath of the war, when I was teaching I applied for promotion, to become a deputy headmaster. And I think I must have the British record. I applied ten times and was turned down every time. Now I was actually - it sounds very boastful - a very good teacher. And the various headmasters I worked under during this spell couldn't understand why I wasn't getting promotion. Years and years later I was at this big 'do' in Parliament House or somewhere in Edinburgh, along with Hugh McDiarmid - ladies stripped to the navel and gentlemen with bands round them, you know - and I was introduced to the Lord Provost. And he said, 'Ah, Mr MacCaig, last time we met you were asking for promotion. And,' he said, 'I was chairman of the Education Committee at that time.' And I said, 'Oh, were you? Is it true' (because several of my headmasters at the time suggested this), 'Is it true that the one who objected to me getting promotion was a minister?' And he said, 'I'm sorry to say it was.' That was ten, fifteen years after the war. So I was victimised in my own profession for years, in the sense of promotion being blocked. And it was the minister who did it.

Norman MacCaig, in Ian MacDougall *Voices from war*

We are proud to call ourselves friends of Faslane Peace Camp

We live in the village of Rhu, about three miles from the Camp, and have been associated with it since day one. What changes we have seen since then! From a small group of people sitting in the long grass under a blazing sun with one tent to the present encampment of brightly painted caravans linked by neat gravel paths, with flower beds, a vegetable plot, running water and flushing toilets and a well laid out information centre.

Many, many people have come and gone, some staying for an hour, some for months. The Camp itself is well established, so much so that it even features on the latest electoral roll with five campers entitled to vote in the elections. Local resistance to and criticisms of the Camp have largely subsided, mainly due to the attitude of the campers themselves. You cannot help but admire their dedication (whatever your views in the nuclear debate) and ability to overcome many obstacles that have been put in their path. The Camp has been subject to vandalism, the campers have been physically assaulted and verbally abused but they have never reacted violently. Their way of handling matters is to sit down and talk or, as in the case of one aggressive visitor bent on damaging them and the camp, to join hands and

Pencil drawing of the West Old Dock, Leith, by Fred Jay Girling, showing floating accommodation and a training ship of the Royal Naval Volunteer Reserve, 1958.

sing. People used to physical violence cannot handle this approach and several have been completely won over.

The support of Dumbarton District and Strathclyde Regional Councils is a unique achievement. Without being strangled by establishment support, this has allowed the camp to get on with the job of promoting peace, rather than being diverted into confrontation with 'vigilante' groups, police and the armed services as with other camps.

Joan and Iain Macdonald, in Faslane Peace Group
Faslane, diary of a peace camp

Nightmares

Since I came back from Burma nearly fifty years ago I've had these terrible nightmares. The war is the source of them because it's all this violent stuff. I'm always fightin' for my life. I'm always retaliatin' or wardin' off or sometimes bein' chased. They're shapes, they're no people in Japanese uniform. They're jist shapes. They've a' got weapons.

I never had nightmares like this when I was in Burma, never, never, never. Because most o' the time when you went to sleep there you were exhausted. You just dropped off to sleep. I've stood on sentry duty, I've stood on watch. I've found that if I've had a rifle I always fixed the bayonet and put it under my chin and stood that way. And if I nodded off I would get it - it's the only way you could keep awake. I'd get a wee cut and it would hit the bone - it would only have a nick, like. But that was to keep awake. It was a trick everybody knew. Aye, a lot o' them did that because you'd maybe gone three or four nights wi' a couple o' hours sleep. And sometimes you'd maybe no' slept properly for days on end, you now, just had an odd forty winks here and there. So if you were standin' to, all these guys were tryin' to steal an hour or two's sleep, it kept you awake just! If you didnae have that you'd be in your foxhole and you'd get your fightin' dagger out and you'd put that under your chin and you would sit like that, watchin'. And when you nodded off... It kept you awake.

So I'm still havin' nightmares about my experiences. I wake up shoutin' or kicking the bedboard sometimes. There was one dreadful occasion four or five years ago when I had my wife Nan by the throat. I've got the thumb round there where I've been trained to put it. That's bad. It's dangerous. That wakened Nan. So I mean she got a terrible fright. And I've never forgotten it. I'm terrified I ever do it again. I'm still pretty strong, you know. On another occasion when I was havin' nightmares I kicked out and I hit the wall with my foot and near broke ma toe. The nightmares are pretty horrible. I wake up wi' the sweat runnin' off me, you know, shakin' like a leaf. Nan's always aware because I'm movin' violently in the bed or I'm sittin' up starin' wi' my eyes, you know. 'Come on, you're OK,' she'll say. And I just go to sleep again.

Eddie Mathieson, in Ian MacDougall *Voices from war*

Combat veterans demand medical help

Scottish veterans last night called for immediate action to help sufferers of Gulf War syndrome following the publication of the pesticides report.

Former soldiers said apologies and resignations from those responsible for misleading information about the use of organophosphates were less important than treatment for victims.

Jim Duncan, Scottish co-ordinator of the National Gulf Veterans and Families Association, said: "It is getting to the stage where there are too many suicides and deaths through illness.

The Government is going to have to do something really quickly, such as get as many veterans tested as possible to find out exactly what is wrong with them and stop them getting any worse."

Mr Duncan, 40, of Invergordon, who was attached to the Scots Guards in the Gulf, has suffered from leukaemia, muscular pain, headaches and memory loss since the conflict and been unable to work.

The Scotsman 27 February 1997

ENVOI

The Black Watch after Waterloo

I trust I shall not be considered egotistical, in saying that I had some narrow escapes this day; but what soldier entered the field, and came safe out of it, had not narrow escapes? A musket-ball struck my halberd in line with my cheek, another passed between my arm and my side and lodged in my knapsack, another struck the handle of my sword, and a fourth passed through my bonnet and knocked it off my head; had the ball been two inches lower, or I that much higher, the reader would have been spared the trouble of reading this narrative.

James Anton *Retrospect of a military life*

Drawing of the memorial to Major General Sir John Campbell, Bart, who died in the Crimea, 1855. NMS

GLOSSARY

abune : above
aefald : simple
aiken : oaken
an : if
anerly : only
auld-farrant : old fashioned
ava : at all

back-end : autumn
bairn : child
bauld : bold
beezed : improved, polished
begrutten : begrudged
behaldand : beholding
ben : through
bide ahint : stay behind
bield : shelter
blate : shy
bogle : ghost
brae : hillside
but-and-ben : two-roomed cottage

caller : fresh
cantie : lively, cheerful
chaulmers : chambers, rooms
chiel : fellow, lad
clapperin : talking, gossiping
clarty : dirty
clout : cloth
crack : chat

daunder : stroll
daur : dare
deil, de'il : devil
delve : dig
dicht : wipe

douce : gentle
dour : hard, severe, stubborn
dowie : sad
dozie : sleepy
draik : quench
drouth : thirst
dule : grief

eident : eager
ettle : strive

feucht : fought
fleg : fright
forlipnin : trusting utterly

gabbin : talking
gang : go
gangrel : vagrant
gar, gart : make, made
gate : way
gear : kit, equipment
gin : if
gled : hawk
gloaming : twilight
greeting : weeping
guddling : tickling

hairst : harvest
hale : whole
happit : covered
heill : shield
heuk : hook
hinny : honey
hirple : limp
housewife : (pronounced 'hussif') sewing kit
howking : digging

ilk, ilka : each

kail-pat : soup pot
kale : cabbage, cabbage soup
kyle : strait
Lallans : Lowlands, a form of Scots
law : hill
lawtie : loyalty
lee : lie
leit : consider
licht : light
lig : lie
loan, loaning : hill
loon : lad
loup : jump
lown : soft
lug : ear
lyart : silvery grey

M O : Medical officer
maist : most
mercat : market
monie : many
mools : earth

ochone : a Gaelic expression of lament
ony : any

paling : fence
pechin : panting
pey : pay
philabeg : kilt
pow : head, brow

quean, queyn : girl

redd : clean
rin : run
rouch : rough

sair : sore, sorely
sauld : sold
saut : salt
shaw : wood
shieling : shelter, poor house
sic : such
skinklin : glittering, sparkling
skreigh : break of day
slock : a hollow, pass
smoor : smother
snowk : sniff
sodger, soger : soldier
sorr : sir
Southeron : the south, England
sowans : a dish prepared from fermented oats
speer : ask, enquire
steek : lock up
stound : swoon
stour : battle, contest
streinyeit : constrained
strenthiast : strongest

tambouring : a type of embroidery
tablet : a confectionery, like hard fudge
tatties : potatoes
tent : care, take care

waucht : gulp, draught
wauk : waken
wean : child
wersh : sour
whiles : sometimes

yett : gate

BIBLIOGRAPHY

ANTON, J. *Retrospect of a military life* Edinburgh: Lizars, and Fraser and Co, 1841

BLACK, J L. *Penicuik and neighbourhood* Edinburgh, n d

BLASER, B. *Kilts across the Jordan: being experiences and impressions with the Second Battalion 'London Scottish' in Palestine* London: H F and G Witherby, 1926

CANNON, R. *Historical records of the Royal Regiment of Scots Dragoons* London: Longman Orme and William Clowes, 1840

COCHRANE, P. *Charlie Company: in service with C Company 2nd Queen's Own Cameron Highlanders, 1940-44* London: Chatto and Windus, 1977

CORBETT, A F. *Service through six reigns; 1891 to 1953* Privately printed, 1953

DÒMHNALLACH, D. *Dòmhnall Ruadh Chorùna* Glasgow, Gairm, 1969

DONALDSON, J. *The eventful life of a soldier* London: Charles Griffin, 1863

DOUGHTY, A. *The Siege of Quebec and the Battle of the Plains of Abraham* Quebec, 1901

EREIRA, A. *The Invergordon mutiny: a narrative history of the last great mutiny in the Royal Navy and how it forced Britain off the Gold Standard in 1931* London: Routledge and Kegan Paul, 1981

Evacuation in Scotland: a record of events and experiments / edited by William Boyd Bickley: University of London Press, 1944

Faslane: diary of a peace camp / by members of the Faslane Peace Group Edinburgh: Polygon Books, 1984

FORMAN, D. *Son of Adam* London: Andre Deutsch, 1990

FRASER, G M. *McAuslan in the rough* London: Barrie and Jenkins, 1974

FRASER, G M. *Quartered safe out here: a recollection of the war in Burma* London: Harvill, 1992

FULLER, J G. *Troop morale and popular culture in the British and Dominion armies, 1914-1918* Oxford: Clarendon Press, 1990

GIBBON, L G. *A Scots quair* London: Jarrolds, 1946

GIBSON, D A. *Now the bell rings: a poet's progress* Galashiels: privately printed, n d

GILCHRIST, D. *Castle Commando* Edinburgh: Oliver and Boyd, 1960

GRANT, E. *Memoirs of a Highland lady* 2 vols Edinburgh: Canongate, 1988

Historical Records of the Cameron Highlanders, Edinburgh: Blackwoods, 1909-62

THE CHEVALIER DE JOHNSTONE *Memoirs of the rebellion in **1745**, 1746* London, 1820

Journal of a soldier of the Seventy-First Regiment, Highland Light Infantry, from 1800 to 1815, including particulars of the Battles of Vimiera, Corunna, Vittoria, The Pyrenees, Toulouse and Waterloo, etc. Edinburgh, 1822

LENEMAN, L. *In the service of life: the story of Elsie Inglis and the Scottish Women's Hospitals*

Edinburgh: Mercat Press, 1994

LOMAX, E. *The railway man* London: Jonathan Cape, 1995

MCCALLUM, N. *Journey with a pistol* London: Gollancz, 1959

MACDOUGALL, I. *The prisoners at Penicuik* Dalkeith: Midlothian District Council, 1989

MACDOUGALL, I. *Voices from the Spanish Civil War* Edinburgh: Polygon, 1986

MACDOUGALL, I. *Voices from war and some labour struggles: personal recollections of war in our century by Scottish men and women* Edinburgh: Mercat Press, 1995

MASTERS, J. *Bugles and a tiger* London: Buchan and Enright, 1956

MENZIES, J. *Reminiscences of an old soldier* Edinburgh: Crawford and McCabe, 1883

NICHOLSON, M. *What did you do in the war, mummy?* London: Chatto, 1995

NIVEN, D. *The moon's a balloon: reminiscences* London: Hamish Hamilton, 1971

Peninsular private edited by Major Eric Robson *Journal of the Society for Army Historical Research* XXXII no 129, 1954, 4-14

Rambling soldier edited by Roy Palmer, Harmondsworth: Penguin, 1977

RAMSAY, Dean *Reminiscences of Scottish life and character* Edinburgh: T N Foulis, 1911

Regimental standing orders, 90th Light Infantry Chatham: James Burrill, 1848

REITH, Lord *Wearing spurs* London: Hutchinson, 1966

RORIE, D. *A medico's luck in the war, being reminiscences of R A M C work with the 51st (Highland) Division* Aberdeen: Milne and Hutchison, 1929

ROSS, I. *Little grey partridge: First World War diary of Ishobel Ross who served with the Scottish Women's Hospitals unit in Serbia* introduced by Jess Dixon, Aberdeen: Aberdeen University Press, 1988

SOMERVILLE, A. *Autobiography of a working man* London: Turnstile Press, 1951 [First published 1848]

TEISSIER DU CROS, J. *Divided loyalties: a Scotswoman in divided France* Edinburgh: Canongate, 1992

Vicissitudes in the life of a Scottish soldier written by himself London: Henry Colburn, 1827

INDEX

ACKNOWLEDGEMENTS

The Editor would like to thank the following for their assistance, both in suggesting contributions and in helping with the rejection process when the original draft proved far too lengthy, and for their help in tracking down illustrations. Ms Dorothy Kidd, Mr Andrew Martin, Mrs Edith Philip, Ms Emma Robinson, Mrs Christina Ross, Mr Jim Wilson, Mr Stephen Wood, all of the National Museums of Scotland, Mr Sandy Buchanan, Mr John S Gibson, Mr Ian MacDougall, Dr Alasdair Maclean, Dr Louise Maguire, Mr Ian Watson of The Herald and the staff of the Scottish Room and the Reference Library, Edinburgh Central Library. Mrs Joyce Smith of the NMS Photographic Service took most of the photographs.

The Publishers and Editor wish to thank the following for kind permission to print copyright material in this anthology:

Canongate Books Limited for *Divided Loyalties* by Janet Teissier du Cros; Jonathan Cape for *The Railway Man* by Eric Lomax; Peter Cochrane for *Charlie Company*; Curtis Brown for *McAuslan in the Rough* by George MacDonald Fraser; The Daily Telegraph for *Aids alert for Kenya troops* by David Graves and Neil Darbyshire, © Telegraph Group Limited, London, 1987; The Scotsman for the extract of 5 March 1991; Andre Deutsch Ltd for *Son of Adam* by Denis Forman, 1990; Jess Dixon for *Little Grey Partridge: First World War Diary of Ishobel Ross*; Edinburgh University Press for *Nocht o' mortal sicht* by Bessie J B MacArthur and *The bull calves* by Naomi Mitchison from *Anthology of Scottish Women Poets* edited by Catherine Kerrigan; Gairm Publications for *Air an Somme* by Domhnall Domhnallach from *Domhnall Ruadh Choruna*; John S Gibson for *Mute with complaint* from *Now the bell rings* by Donald A Gibson; Donald Gilchrist and the Lochaber Area Committee of The Highland Council for *Castle Commando*; Hamish Hamilton for *The Moon's a Balloon* by David Niven; Hamish Henderson for *51st (Highland) Division's Farewell to Sicily*; HarperCollins Publishers Ltd for *Quartered Safe Out Here* by George MacDonald Fraser; The Highlander for the obituary of Lieutenant Colonel Jack Churchill DSO MC; Mrs Mary Hill and the Trustees of the National Library of Scotland for George Campbell Hay's letter to Douglas Young; Leah Leneman for *In the service of life: the story of Elsie Inglis and the Scottish Women's Hospitals*, Mercat Press; Ian MacDougall for *Voices from the Spanish Civil War* and *Voices from War*; His Grace the Duke of Northumberland for the journal of Serjeant John Wilson; excerpts from *Troop morale and popular culture in the British and Dominion armies, 1914-18*, by J G Fuller (1990), by permission of Oxford University Press; Polygon for *Faslane, Diary of a peace camp* by Faslane Peace Group; Random House UK Ltd for *Wearing Spurs* by Lord Reith, published by Hutchinson; Routledge for *The Invergordon Mutiny* pp 9 and 63, by Alan Ereira, 1981; the Trustees of the National Library of Scotland for *Hal o' the Wynd* by William Soutar; University of London Press/Hodder & Stoughton Educational Ltd for William Boyd Bickley (ed) *Evacuation in Scotland*; A P Watt Ltd on behalf of The Lord Tweedsmuir and Lady Tweedsmuir for *Home Thoughts from Abroad (1917)* by John Buchan.

All our attempts at tracing the copyright holder of *Kilts across the Jordan* by Bernard Blaser, published by Victor Gollancz, were unsuccessful.

Every effort has been made to trace the copyright holders of the works included in this anthology. If any error or oversight has occurred the Publishers will be grateful for information, and will correct any such errors at the earliest opportunity.